The Entrepreneur's Guide to Hiring and Building the Team

The Entrepreneur's Guide

CJ Rhoads, Series Editor

The Entrepreneur's Guide to Hiring and Building the Team

Ken Tanner

Westport, Connecticut
London

Library of Congress Cataloging-in-Publication Data

Tanner, Ken.
  The entrepreneur's guide to hiring and building the team / Ken Tanner.
    p. cm. — (The entrepreneur's guide, ISSN 1939–2478)
  Includes bibliographical references and index.
  ISBN 978–0–275–99543–0 (alk. paper)
  1. Teams in the workplace. 2. Employees—Recruiting. I. Title. II. Series.
  HD66.T365 2008
  658.4′022—dc22   2007036487

British Library Cataloguing in Publication Data is available.

Library of Congress Catalog Card Number: 2007036487
ISBN: 978–0–275–99543–0
ISSN: 1939–2478

First published in 2008

Praeger Publishers, 88 Post Road West, Westport, CT 06881
An imprint of Greenwood Publishing Group, Inc.
www.praeger.com

Printed in the United States of America

∞™

The paper used in this book complies with the
Permanent Paper Standard issued by the National
Information Standards Organization (Z39.48–1984).

10 9 8 7 6 5 4 3 2 1

For my father, Stan Tanner, who, along with fellow members
of his generation, conquered poverty during the Depression,
defeated evil during a world war, led our nation to previously
unimaginable levels of productivity and prosperity, selflessly raised a
new generation of leaders, and then quietly stepped aside to
look back at a life well led.

Contents

Acknowledgments

Immediately after signing the contract for this book—my fourth—I decided to hire one of those interns I had heard so much about. I conducted a series of conversations (not interviews) and chose Lauren Azzalina to be my researcher, fact-checker, and first-draft copy editor.

Let me tell you a little bit about this remarkable young woman. Lauren was a recent graduate of Valdosta State University and eager to start her career. As with most English majors, that career began in the back of a restaurant, a job she continued to hold for the early months of her service to me. Lauren then added yet another internship, this time with an outstanding publishing house in Atlanta. Lauren soon moved from a restaurant to a reception desk greeting students at a prestigious dance studio.

Despite juggling multiple jobs and internships, Lauren produced quality work, learned a lot, and built a solid reputation in the business community. How solid? She completed the publishing internship with the highest possible evaluation, and the dance studio promoted her to the position of head administrator.

So I acknowledge the significant contributions Lauren Azzalina made. Her work, advice, and perspectives have been critical to the development of this book; I thank her. However, I need to do more than acknowledge her contributions to this book. I must also acknowledge the promise she shows. Just like the entrepreneurs now reading these words, Lauren displays that magical combination of talents, skills, persistence, and optimism. Her future is so very bright; it will be a joy to watch it evolve.

Introduction

Sam was a new client. We were sharing a pot of coffee as he described the moment he decided to leave his long-time employer and start his own company:

> My boss had just returned from one of those teambuilding retreats. You know, one of those deals where the top brass go into the wilderness for the weekend, have paintball wars, walk on burning coals, and then sit around a campfire singing Kumbaya?

I was familiar with the concept. Indeed, conducting such retreats is a good income stream for me. I was often able to build real team spirit among executives with exercises done off-campus, though my methods had never included weapons, fire, or (*shudder!*) karaoke. He continued:

> So the boss calls us all together to summarize what he had learned. After a lot of interesting stories about the athletic prowess (or lack thereof) of some of the other division heads, he reviewed some of the planning they had done. They had identified future markets, product opportunities, and opportunities for cost cutting.

Again, I nodded. I have seen wonderful results from these meetings. You break down some of the communication barriers executives have built and the team can produce excellent planning.

> And then he told us about an interesting exercise. As a group, they ranked the company's most important strengths, its most valuable assets. "Our greatest asset," he declared, "is cash." Someone interrupted him and said he'd always heard that people were our greatest asset. "Where do people rank on the new list?" he asked. The boss studied his notes and replied, "Sixteenth. People are now considered sixteenth." I had to ask him what fifteenth was. "Our solid inventory of office supplies and equipment," he replied. From that moment, I knew I had to get out of a corporate system that valued paperclips over its people.

Let's at least give this company credit for not being hypocritical. Companies loudly proclaim that they value their people, but few believe it and even fewer live it. "Our people are our greatest asset" has become a business cliché. However, there is a reason a phrase evolves into a cliché and that is because of its truth. Committed, motivated, and productive people are the organization's heartbeat. Their quality decides whether it thrives or turns to dust.

There are few absolute truths in business, but here is one: The success or failure of your entrepreneurial business can be predicted by the quality of the people you bring into it. Your new company will flourish or flounder depending how well you recruit, build, and retain your team.

Yet, there is an even stronger reason for you to have a great team. That lies in the same basic advice I give job seekers. When deciding between job offers, I advise them to look closely at the people in the organizations. I tell them, "You become your environment." You, too, will become whomever you choose to associate with.

Take great care in the selection of your team members, because your business will reflect their DNA: their character, work ethic, talents, strengths—all these things will become the character of your business. You will be whatever your people are.

The Entrepreneur's Guide to Hiring and Building the Team will help you possess this great team. We'll discover ways for you to recruit the talent best suited for your business and learn how to mold these assets into a powerful team. Most importantly, we'll explore proven methods to conquer turnover and keep this great team together.

You've heard all that before, haven't you? The bookstores are filled with such claims; let's see how this book is different.

Recruiting. Existing titles only address the *hiring* aspect of recruiting and most of those are composed of a list of "great interview questions." Actually, the questions really aren't that great, just tricky ones that serve to make the candidate nervous and guarded. *Hiring and Building the Team* guides you through the *entire* arena of recruiting, including preparation, sourcing, selection, and onboarding, in addition to the interview process.

Teambuilding. Most teambuilding books consist of clever games you can play with your staff. These make for entertaining meetings, but teach nothing about how to build a solid, focused team that will further your fledgling business. This book shows how to build teams and make them work. From identifying each person's role to measuring accountability to triumphing over obstacles, *Hiring and Building the Team* will show you how to get these talented people to work together to drive your business.

Retention. Most books about employee retention—wait, there really aren't many books on the subject. Those that can be found discuss how to keep the employee smiling, laughing, and motivated for the short-term, while ignoring basic concepts for holding on to each individual member of the team you have created. *Hiring and Building the Team* shows how to keep each employee challenged, motivated, and satisfied. You will know how to address each person's true needs and keep them for the long-term.

You are also wondering why you should look to Ken Tanner for this guidance when the bookstores offer advice directly from a plethora of PhDs, sports celebrities, and even The Donald himself! So, why should you trust me to take you on this journey? Fair question. Let me tell you a little about myself.

While I never served as president of General Motors, invented the Internet, or cured any major diseases (at least none that you would immediately recognize), chances are you wouldn't relate to me if I had. Unlike many of the golden gurus who dispense career advice from atop an ivory pedestal, my route to the top included slogging through trenches, taking some detours, enduring tons of confusion, and falling into numerous potholes. The other gurus offer you glamour, notoriety, even some interesting hair, but my career experience is probably closer to the one you are having right now. You and I can talk.

I won't lay out my résumé, but I have had a pretty solid business career. My "first career" included service at all levels of management for small regional companies, international giants, and most points in between. I've had my own entrepreneurial ventures, headed nonprofit organizations (most were even that way on purpose), as well as having my own consulting practice for the past dozen years. My past titles include national director of training, regional director, and executive vice president, as well as dishwasher, disc jockey, and dog walker. I've had my struggles, victories, and all points in between.

My vehicle for professional success has not been an Ivy League education, family connections, or even a magnetic personality. It was certainly not my good looks. My great strength is the ability to recruit, motivate, and develop amazing people. This talent compensates for my many frailties. It has also prepared me to write this book for you.

Let me share a personal insight I had while writing this book: I eagerly signed the contract to write *Hiring and Building the Team* because I was sure it would be quick and easy to produce. After all, I had already written books on recruiting as well as employee retention. Converting them to this project seemed to be easy work indeed. I soon realized that the entrepreneur faces a different paradigm than MegaGlobal Intergalactic, Inc. (You will be relieved to know this is the only time I will use the word *paradigm* in this book.) You don't have the same resources as Ford. Your problems are not the same as Delta's. Your goals, ambitions, culture—none of your issues match those of a large corporation. The good advice I give large corporate clients is lousy advice for you. Your unique challenges deserve customized solutions. That is exactly what I want to give you in this book.

This individualized support does not end on the last page. I respect the courage you show by being an entrepreneur and will be proud to help you with this journey. Contact me at kentanner@consultant.com and we'll talk.

RECRUITING YOUR TEAM

We all have our dreams, don't we? Unlike most middle-aged men, my fantasy is to be awarded an expansion franchise for major league baseball. I fanaticize about the first steps I'll take right after writing the commissioner the (rubber) check.

Sometimes I ponder the name of the team. Other times, I start with designing the uniforms. Perhaps the most enjoyment comes from trying to think of all the ways I can extort the city into building me a free stadium. After all the silly stuff, I'll get down to considering the most important issue: How do I get the best players? How do I determine my needs, identify the really good players, and then convince them to play on my team—at a reasonable salary?

My fantasy is your reality. As an entrepreneur, you are bringing your dream into existence. You know that nothing is more critical to your success than surrounding yourself with great people. You are asking yourself the same questions I do as I build my baseball team. Only for you, this is real.

This section explores recruiting, the first element of having a great team. Let's learn how to attract the people we both must have to assure our success and achieve our dreams.

Preparing to Recruit

My Mom was famous for her coconut cake, a secret family recipe that was handed down from her grandmother. One day a dear friend somehow found the right words to convince her to share the recipe for the friend's anniversary dinner.

Mom was excited to attend the dinner and see her famous cake produced from someone else's kitchen. Just before the premiere, the friend pulled her aside and confided that she had made a few changes in the recipe. She confessed she had used canned pineapple instead of fresh, reduced the number of egg yolks from five to three. ("That's all I had handy," she sheepishly admitted.) She also forgot about the pecans. What about the *coup de grace*? The coconut came from a bag that was buried in the back of the freezer. Mom trembled as she returned to the table.

Her jaw hit the tabletop when her friend brought the imitation pineapple coconut cake to the table and announced to her assembled friends and family: "If you don't like the cake, don't blame me. It's Blanche's recipe!"

Hiring the best people does not happen by accident. Heck, nothing excellent ever happens by accident. Great results come only after quality preparation and by following a carefully crafted plan.

You know this. Although if you have the typical profile of an entrepreneur, your first urge is to dive right in and get it done. While this trait can serve you well in many other business situations, it will destroy your efforts to build a team.

Overcome the urge to skip this chapter and dive right into the "good stuff." Let me assure you, there will be no good stuff if you don't prepare properly. For this process to work, you must follow four critical steps for preparing to recruit.

CRITICAL PREPARATION STEP 1: RECOGNIZE THAT MOST PEOPLE WOULD RATHER WORK FOR SMALL COMPANIES

Small companies feel they have a hiring handicap. They believe that it is difficult to hire quality people because prize candidates prefer to work for the big guys. This feeling of inferiority often causes entrepreneurs to fear going after top candidates, often settling for second-rate talent. That is, of course, a formula for disaster.

Here is the good news: This perception is wrong. Not only can you compete with the corporate giants for good people, you often have the *advantage* in that competition. We will discuss this in some detail in Section III, but the secret to retaining—and hiring people—is this: Find out what their needs are and meet those needs. Here is the good news: small companies are in a better position to address employees' needs than large ones are.

Fact: Most people would rather work for a smaller firm.
Fact: Many top-notch candidates prefer you to industry giants.
Fact: You can hire the best.

You must convince yourself of these facts before you can confidently sell candidates on your company. Since your future is so directly tied to employing first-rate people, we're going to explore this issue in some depth. Why should a candidate be more excited working for you than MegaGlobal? Let's look at the many ways you meet their needs.

You Can Directly Address the Employees' Needs

Simply put, people want their needs met and you are better able to meet those needs. While this is discussed in detail in Section III, let's first take a top-line look at how you can address those needs better than MegaGlobal can.

The Need for Security

The dot.com bust of the 1990s caused a serious misconception among security-motivated workers, chasing many security-conscious workers away from smaller or entrepreneurial companies. Contrary to this public image, a smaller organization often provides greater job security than the corporate giants. This is most dramatically seen in layoffs. Large corporations often use reorganizations, mass layoffs, and firings as a tool to drive stock prices. (Isn't it interesting how many companies announce massive layoffs, see their stock prices rise, and then begin a massive hiring program soon thereafter?) Entrepreneurial companies do not engage in such nonsense. Further, since smaller companies have closer relations with their workers, layoffs are last resorts rather than being cold-blooded impersonal actions the corporate giants are prone to whip out.

The Need to Feel Special

Here is why it is easier to make your workers feel more valuable than MegaGlobal can make theirs: *they are*. Also, they know they are, but you can also take it a step farther. Many people are title- or status-motivated. Large company executives are locked in to their job titles, but you don't have to be. Make your sales manager the Director of Sales. Your receptionist can become Hospitality Coordinator, a bookkeeper turns into the Records Manager, and so on. (Think this is insignificant? Picture what would happen to egos if the military removed symbols of rank from the uniforms.) You have tremendous flexibility for using this tool; don't let it escape you. (It also helps a former salesman explain to his wife why he left MegaGlobal to become a sales manager for you.)

The Need to Feel Needed

Being just another cog in the corporate machine makes employees feel their efforts have no impact, no meaning. However, every employee action has a direct and immediate impact in your company. Employees know that their full talents and contributions are critical to your company's success. This is no small thing. People crave meaning in their lives; for many, the worst torture is to live a life with no significance. You can provide that; MegaGlobal cannot.

The Need to Have Control

When a large company has hundreds of people doing the same type of job, they must understandably dictate all methods and steps in how that job must be performed. When your employee is the only person doing the job, she can take great latitude in her methods. She can shape the procedures to fit her skills. She feels more in control.

The Need for Influence

Employees of smaller companies know each other. If an employee sees a needed change, he will know exactly who to go to in order to immediately implement the change. This includes the CEO, who, unlike senior management at large companies, is approachable and involved with employees on a regular basis. Your employees are more empowered than their counterparts at the big companies and this makes their jobs richer.

You Offer a Better Culture

Many workers spend more of their waking hours in their office than their home. They spend more time with their co-workers than their family. Your potential employees, especially those in mid-career, recognize this. You can offer top candidates a work environment and culture which appeals to many workers. Here are some of those ways:

You Offer a Healthier Atmosphere

Petty politics thrives where there is a huge bureaucracy, shallow peer relationships, and distant management. By definition, smaller companies see less petty politics. Good candidates, particularly those who are fed up with the backstabbing in their present company, will eagerly leave a poisonous corporate atmosphere to work in your atmosphere.

Your Employees Understand the Vision

They are the most important part of that vision. Big corporations have a culture that is often distant from the actual vision of top management. In small companies, everybody works together where the owner's vision, integrity, and passion creates a similar culture for employees. Also, because smaller companies have more line-of-sight management, the CEO will often work side-by-side with employees at every level.

Communication Flows More Efficiently

"Poor communications" is usually in the top three complaints when I do a company culture survey. The larger the company, the higher this ranks. The people in sales have no clue what's happening in operations. Information circulates via e-mail, memoranda, and rumor, if at all. That's not an issue in a small operation of five, ten, or twenty employees, where you can gather everyone around the coffeepot for timely updates.

You Offer Less Bureaucracy

Decisions are made more quickly at smaller companies and the people who make them are usually two doors down rather than across the ocean. Plus, if an employee decides something needs changing, she knows exactly who to speak with to make it happen immediately.

You Provide Better Career Development

While many people crave the pedigree that giant corporations offer their résumé, you can offer career development opportunities that are unmatched by larger companies.

You Offer More Opportunity

When hiring for a position, big companies use a strict template. For instance, a director of marketing must have a marketing degree, maybe even an MBA, x years of total experience and x years working for a pedigreed firm. Lots of outstanding people fall out of these arbitrary templates. MegaGlobal cannot bend, but you most certainly can.

You Provide More Hats

Being a smaller organization, you can be more flexible in your job descriptions than large companies. In fact, in many cases you can actually shape the job around the person. You can match their experience, talents, and interests with your company's needs. For instance, you may have a bookkeeper that also has an interest and talent in marketing. You could easily allow her to be involved in marketing decisions and even consider executing her marketing ideas. Indeed, this concept of wearing a lot of hats is common in smaller companies that are prone to draw on talent where it exists and is a definite advantage you can offer potential employees. They could never get this type of exposure, experience, or involvement working for a large company.

You Provide Better Mentoring

Smaller companies have more line-of-sight management with employees working alongside experienced people, including the CEO. Mentoring relationships form more quickly and are of a high quality. Large corporations may offer mentorship programs, but these are often more engineered associations that do not offer the depth of those that develop through natural interaction.

You Provide a Better Opportunity for Moving Up

True, large companies have more levels, more departments, and a greater number of positions an employee can possibly move into, but they also have tremendous competition for those spots. Here is what you offer in that regard: the employee will get much greater exposure to all the processes and decisions, as well as participating at a higher level in the decision-making process sooner in his career. This education will prepare him for more responsibility more quickly than if he worked at MegaGlobal.

You provide richer career development than the big companies. Embrace this fact and you will have the confidence to recruit strong candidates.

CRITICAL PREPARATION STEP 2: DETERMINE YOUR NEEDS

You are proud of how your business has been growing. Sales continue to increase at a nice, steady pace, cash flow is solid, and the future looks good. Things are looking bright, indeed. What doesn't look good is your ability to continue working sixteen-hour days. Your current employees, while still enthusiastic, aren't too keen about continuing to shoulder a similar workload. You need help.

Established companies think of the hiring process as something that is done when an employee quits. Entrepreneurs view it from a different perspective. Hiring is done as a natural part of the growth process for a fledgling business. While replacement hiring has many factors to consider, hiring for growth brings a few more elements to the table. These two questions must be initially considered: When do you add staff and what types of positions need to be added? Let's look at some of the events that may indicate it is time to expand your workforce.

Your Current Employees Are Screaming "Uncle!"

When large amounts of overtime become routine and ongoing, it is an indication that you need more people. Excess overtime is financially inefficient and will lead to worker burnout. Employees who are routinely overloaded will be under-productive. Call for reinforcements before your workers burn out.

But your employees aren't the only ones risking burnout; you may be as well. There are only twenty-four hours in a day, no matter how hard you work. Even though you may love the hard work, there is a point where your business will suffer because of it. When you start dropping balls that you formerly juggled with ease, spend more time with crises rather than daily operations, or are unable to find the time to attract new customers, it is time to increase your workforce.

Opportunity Is Calling

Your sales continue to grow and you determine this is a trend, not a blip. You see great opportunity in expanding into a new market, new city, or even a new product line. Whatever the specifics, it is time to add staff when you determine an opportunity exists that your current workforce cannot handle.

Your Sales Backlog Is Growing

Order backlogs signal the need for extra help. The fact that orders are available indicates that additional labor would fund itself. Even if the backlog does not by itself justify increasing your staffing, it may indicate the potential for more business if you had the manpower to fill it. (Perhaps your sales team has backed off, not wanting to develop sales that would be filled in an untimely manner.)

Customer Service Is Suffering

Satisfied customers are repeat customers; unhappy ones do not hesitate to knock on your competitor's door. Take an honest look at how you are serving your existing customers. Are you meeting their expectations? Extra staff could boost their satisfaction and attract new business.

Talent Is Available

You are willing to invest in new real estate to address future market conditions. You purchase new equipment if it brings strategic advantages. Why not approach your investment in people in the same way?

Perhaps a formerly retired industry leader shows interest in joining your organization, a competitor has to lay off several highly skilled machinists, or a talented salesperson with a long list of client relationships becomes available. Sometimes you must bend your timetable to take advantage of talent availability.

More to Ponder before You Expand

So, should you expand your staff? Here are some additional questions to help you make that decision:

- Is your existing team performing necessary, value-producing work, or are there some tasks that can be eliminated/outsourced, allowing them to concentrate on their real tasks?
- Conversely, if this is a newly-created staff function, is there an existing worker with expertise/interest in this new role who could expand his or her job?
- How much will revenue increase with the added employee? (A good rule of thumb is to require an increase of three times the added expense.)
- What is your current revenue per employee? What will it be with the added worker? The number will initially go down, of course, but you should demand a long-term increase.

Alternate Strategies Instead of Adding New Staff

There are other ways to add workers without expanding your payroll. Let's look at some of these options.

Outsource to Other Businesses

Here is a good rule of thumb: hire an employee if the work is part of your core service. (You want to maintain control of the product being provided to your customer.) If it's a secondary function that does not respond directly to the customer (such as bookkeeping, janitorial, or Web site maintenance) it may be more cost-effective to outsource. Also, it is a drain on your focus to manage functions not related to your core business. Consider outsourcing any function outside of your expertise.

Outsource to Your Customer

What do self-service gas pumps, ATMs, self-serve soda stations, and bag-your-own grocery stations have in common? They are all examples of businesses that reduced their need for labor by letting customers do part of the work.

IKEA is another great example of this. They sell unassembled furniture that customers must put together when they get home. Customers have no objection because the work is quite simple (usually, just screwing four legs into a table), instructions are clear, and the prices are outrageously low. There are two reasons for the low prices: The labor savings is significant, but the company also enjoys significant savings in shipping costs.

Temp Agencies

For certain positions, especially office and accounting roles, temping is a way to obtain quality help with little hassle. Working with a temp allows you to tweak the new position as well as provide a risk-free way to see if you actually need to add the position permanently. If you decide the position is unnecessary, it is quite simple to discontinue the service. On the other hand, if the new position seems valuable, then there is a good chance you already have the right person working for you. (Tread cautiously: temp agencies charge a hefty fee if you hire one of their workers full-time.)

Use Independent Contractors

Classifying certain workers as "independent contractors" may present an opportunity for saving some money. You do not have to pay these workers' insurance, taxes, or employee benefits. Despite this possible opportunity, I rarely recommend this option. Classifying an employee as an independent contractor provides some serious risks as well as a loss of control. In a true subcontractor relationship, you have little control over how people do their work. Losing this control could be disastrous to your company. However, keeping this control while also classifying a worker as an "independent contractor" runs the risk of legal violations and severe financial penalties.

An independent contractor can be useful for performing non-routine tasks, such as delivering catalogs or preparing a one-time special project. However, do not use this designation for any function that is *central* to your business. If yours is an accounting firm, do not classify your accountants as independent contractors. You must maintain full control of your core product. Again, tread cautiously. The small financial benefits derived from this employment status are rarely worth the potential headaches.

CRITICAL PREPARATION STEP 3: ACCURATELY ASSESS THE SITUATION

Now you have made the decision to hire another worker. Whom should you hire? You will hire the person who is best suited to your business, of course. How do you determine who is the best suited? Your first reaction to these questions is that you will determine this at the interview. However, before you can decide whether the candidate is a good match for the job, you must first determine what it is you are trying to match the employee to.

Job mismatch is a common theme throughout this book and the biggest reason for turnover. While this usually applies to the *type* of work being done, it can equally apply to the workplace itself. Because we place such a heavy emphasis on a candidate's qualifications for the *job*, exploring that candidate's match for the company is often completely overlooked. We must do our best to assure the candidate is a good fit for both the job and your company.

Understand that getting a good fit does not mean an organization of clones. (In fact, as we'll see in Chapter 6, that causes an even greater disaster.) Instead, we are simply ensuring that there's nothing about your organization that would create a square peg/round hole situation. When you interview the candidates, you will be able to assess their responses and see how well they truly match your situation.

Assess Your Culture

The employee must fit in your culture, or at least be able to operate comfortably in it. List things that are important to your company's culture: its mission, values, and characteristics. Here are some examples:

- Everyone's opinion is valued and solicited when we make big decisions.
- Never argue with your boss.
- We are open, direct—even blunt—in our discussions.
- We will do whatever is necessary to settle a customer complaint.
- Work is supposed to be fun.
- We do things by the book.
- Everyone is given great latitude in how he or she performs his or her job.

Note that many of these values are negative. Remember, this is not a document you publish in your PR press releases. It is a tool you will use to determine how well a candidate will fit in with your company. Knowing your values—even the disappointing ones—helps you decide a potential employee's chances of career success.

Assess Your Existing Team

Think about your current employees. Analyze their dynamics, especially their personalities, quirks, and working style. Study the group's interaction. What are the factors that make them work well together and where is there conflict? What kind of person will fit into the positive characteristics of the group? Who could serve to ease conflict or break through logjams?

A new employee will change the dynamic of your existing group. How well you understand your current team will determine whether this is a good thing or feels like hell on a bad day.

CRITICAL PREPARATION STEP 4: DEVELOP THE JOB DESCRIPTION

How often have you seen a smart, energetic, high-quality professional absolutely crash and burn in their new job? Regrettably, this happens often. In fact, the single biggest reason for employee turnover, both voluntary and involuntary, is job mismatch. The biggest reason that people fail in their jobs is that they were never a match for the job in the first place. Job mismatch is a guaranteed route to disaster for the employee as well as for you.

How does this mismatch occur? On the employee's side, it happens because they are unemployed and the mortgage payment is due next week. Because they are desperate, they convince themselves that the first job that comes along is a great opportunity.

However, for the employer, mismatch occurs because he never really understood what the job was or the type of person that would thrive in that role. He didn't do his homework. *The only way to hire the right employee is to understand what makes an employee right.*

So, don't think of writing a job description as one of those bureaucratic, paper-pushing tasks you gave up when you started your own business. It is not bureaucracy; it is a great planning tool. By going through the exercise, you will have a clearer understanding of the job you want to fill and what qualifications are really needed. In fact, writing a job description drives the entire recruiting process. Treat this process with respect.

Here is another benefit of writing a job description: Doing so forces you to closely examine the role of *all the other jobs* already existing in your organization. If you are still small enough, you may find that you can define the roles of existing personnel. You will find that, over time, these roles have evolved unofficially. This is a good time to make those evolutions official. Doing so may result in a need quite different than the one you were originally considering. Perhaps the receptionist has become a computer whiz and is already performing some of the IT needs that you were looking for in the "new guy." Take advantage of this opportunity to shape jobs around people you already know and whose abilities you have confidence in.

Writing the Job Description

Let's go through the thought process for developing a good job description. I've included a sample for a good one, but realize it is just that, an example. Choose your own format to best meet your needs.

Title

Titles are deceiving. You can't rely on them to explain the true nature or scope of the job. For instance, I have seen *Vice Presidents of Operations* who were overseeing one location and I have seen *General Managers* responsible for billion-dollar regions. Don't rely on a title to convey a job's responsibilities. Instead, use them for internal identification or to lure wavering candidates who are title-motivated.

Scope of Responsibilities

The first part of the job description is an honest summary of what the employee will actually be doing. This may seem obvious, but you will be surprised how many people can't describe their job in a sentence or two. Strip the position down to its basics to reduce confusion.

List three to five of the most important duties that make up at least 75 percent of where the person will be expected to focus his time. Then, explain how this performance will be evaluated.

Next, decide who his boss will be. Describe the relationship and how he will be managed. Spend some time on this, especially defining whether the new employee will be closely supervised, work independently, or (more probably) somewhere in between. Be accurate in this to avoid tragic mismatch. Combat soon follows when you place a "take charge person" in a relationship with a boss hovering over his shoulder.

Perhaps you should also explain the approval process for various levels of decisions. For many positions, it would be appropriate to define the person's purchasing authority.

Job Qualifications

There is great danger lurking when you prepare this section. That is because we too often just start listing a lot of boilerplate items that seem to fit the situation and often arbitrarily insert tangent skills. We might also start listing skills that the previous occupant had regardless of whether they were necessary to do the job. (Example: Your last bookkeeper was a member of a professional society. Is that society really necessary to do the job?)

Here is a way to shape the character of the job without placing unreasonable requirements on potential candidates. Divide the job qualifications into two groups, required and desired. Required items are just that—absolute qualifications any candidate must have in order to do the job. Lacking any one of these would be an absolute disqualification and the applicant would receive no further consideration. Examples might be:

- Must be twenty-one years of age in order to work as a bartender.
- Delivery driver must have a clean driving record.
- Salesperson must be available for heavy travel.
- Director of accounting must be a CPA.

A second category should also be created called "desired qualifications." These are qualifications you would like to see but are not absolutely necessary. For instance, using the previous example, you may decide that while you would like your director of accounting to be a CPA, it is not absolutely necessary. In that case, move "CPA" from *required* to *desired*.

While you should be frugal in your list of *required qualifications* (always keep in mind that a candidate will be rejected if he is missing any of those listed), you can be quite expansive in listing *desired qualifications*. A long list of desired traits helps the potential candidate capture a flavor of the job and what you are looking for in an ideal candidate. She'll know that she will be given "extra credit" for all the traits she does have and given the opportunity to explain how she can compensate for those she may be missing.

Personal Traits

Finally, make a list of the ideal candidate's personal traits, such as thrives under pressure, has a positive attitude, and enjoys working in a diverse workforce. This is important because quite often it is a personality mismatch rather than a job mismatch that reduces a person's ability to be effective on the job.

Improve Your Pool of Job Candidates by *Lowering* Your Standards

Sometimes we outsmart ourselves when composing job postings. We want to hire only the best people so we put together a list of qualifications that require stellar credentials. We'll demand an MBA—from an Ivy League school, no doubt—ten years experience, even a job-history pedigree that includes only the most prestigious companies. The result? A job few people qualify for.

Does the job really *require* an MBA? Must the ideal candidate have ten years' experience? Must the person have their degree in journalism? If you require such things, you will eliminate many people who excel in areas you did not list. You may very well eliminate someone who has exceptional people skills, is a brilliant salesman, or has a long list of loyal clients. He "only" has a bachelor's degree, or just seven years' experience, so he doesn't even bother to inquire.

Another limiting requirement has to do with specific degree programs. I've seen trade journals, for instance, look to hire a writer and demanding a degree in journalism. Require? That requirement just eliminated all the outstanding writers with business degrees who also may have many years of experience in that trade along with a plethora of industry contacts!

The solution? Feel free to list "desired" credentials and state that you value these high achievements. However, also make it clear that you welcome inquiries from everyone who thinks he can perform brilliantly for you. Then insist he clearly explain why he would thrive as your employee.

Develop your own list and make sure it accurately describes the traits needed to fit into your company and the specific job. That may be easier said than done; there are some real traps awaiting you in this exercise.

Avoid the temptation to create a boy-scout profile, you know, *trustworthy, loyal, helpful, friendly, courteous*, etc. You are wasting your time if you do this. The only job these traits really match are, well, a boy scout. Realize that most jobs actually need a person holding some traits that may not be so positive. Examples? Good executives are often impatient. Many top-notch sales managers are unreasonably demanding. Do you really want your debt collector to be compassionate?

Also, beware of trait-clichés. For instance, companies declare they want a candidate who is *ambitious*. An ambitious person will quickly become frustrated if you have a small company offering little room for promotion.

How about *aggressive*? Companies say they want to hire aggressive people (what they really mean is *assertive*, by the way). An aggressive person will alienate your entire team if it is a tight knit group or a family-style culture. Take care in what you ask for; make sure it really is what you want.

Also, understand that some traits, even good ones, cannot be combined. Here is an example of a dysfunctional combination: a dedicated team player and someone who is competitive. Competitive people are not team players. Pick one.

A LAST WORD AS YOU PREPARE TO RECRUIT

An eye-opening moment occurs during my retention workshops. I will ask each person to list the reasons they terminated their last five workers. I'll write these reasons on a whiteboard and get multiple responses for reasons such as attendance, attitude, poor people-skills, and dishonesty. Dozens of responses will be on the board, yet only rarely will any of these include job skills. So, even though job skills are rarely reasons for termination, they usually make up the predominate qualifications on a job description. That contradiction causes problems. Technical skills can be taught. Attitude cannot.

If a customer-first attitude is important to you, then put it high up in your job description. If dependability and punctuality are critical, say so. When you interview candidates, make sure you question them on exactly these points.

Like all splendid recipes, excellent recruiting absolutely requires great preparation. Take short cuts, you will lose. Skimp on the research, you will fail. Shortchange the preparation stage, you will get horrid results. Invest your time in the steps I've laid out in this chapter. The results will be worth the effort. On the other hand, if you choose to ignore my recipe, don't blame me for the results.

2

Finding Great Candidates

Time magazine reports of a recruiting extravaganza held in an Atlanta sports venue. Dozens of corporate recruiters for entry-level companies were trying to attract applicants by offering sports and movie tickets in an exciting dynamic venue. In the past, this type of event would ensure the companies could hire all the workers they needed, but not today. Recruiters left with their needs unmet.

The article discusses the terrible time companies have staffing their businesses. It speaks most directly about the entry-level and lower-paying positions normally filled by younger workers, but concludes with remarks by Walter Cadette, an economist from Morgan Guaranty Trust: "McDonald's and Burger King's shortages today will be General Motors' and IBM's shortages tomorrow." Mr. Cadette's prophecy became reality as his words were spoken. The date of the article? April 1986.

Since the end of World War II, our booming economy has always had plenty of labor. Returning soldiers took care of the need through the 1970s. Then, just as our economy began to really explode, the numerous baby boomers, along with the mass entrance of women into the workplace, ensured that manpower would never become a roadblock to economic growth.

However, the baby boomers are beginning to retire. Because my generation did such a lousy job at reproducing, we now see the beginnings of a labor shortage extending across all skill levels and types of professions. This event will pick up tremendous momentum through 2011 and escalate to critical proportions.

My belief is that it will take many years, maybe even a decade, before we learn how to deal with the issue. We will probably address the crisis through a combination of new technologies, global outsourcing, and immigration. That's really just a lot of theory, isn't it? You aren't interested in where we'll get 20 million workers late in the second decade of the twenty-first century, you just want to replace the guy on the loading dock *right now*.

While we do have to accept the fact that the workforce is shrinking, we do not have to settle for second best and let it slow our growth. Be aware of the dramatic impact on your customer base and candidate pool, but do not think that you can only get your "fair share" of the pool. So, how do we capture a greater portion of this dwindling pool? You will win that battle by casting a wide net.

CASTING A WIDE NET

Casting a wide net does not involve treating people like a school of fish. Quite the opposite, it means evaluating people individually, considering each one's potential for your business. It means using multiple recruiting methods to find those wonderfully unique people for your operation. It means knowing that reaching out to a diverse applicant pool leads to the most successful placements. Casting a wide net simply means you want to attract as many potential candidates as possible. You can't hire people you never meet.

There is a drought of quality candidates and it will only get worse. (Actually, there is also a shortage of *unqualified* workers.) You must get more than your share of these workers to survive. Here are three key attitudes that will help you do this:

Be Flexible

If you are hiring for a full-time position but find a great candidate who is only available part-time, consider a job-sharing arrangement or redefine the position. While your company is small, you have the luxury of shaping the job to the person. This flexibility allows you to build an organization based on great people rather than boilerplate rules.

As we discussed in the last chapter, don't limit the pool by requiring inflexible qualifications, such as "ten years experience." Must they have ten years? Do you really want to eliminate the ones with nine years? Four years? Two?

Flexibility is one of the great advantages an entrepreneur has over the industry giants. Make full use of it.

Use Diverse Sources

Excellent recruiting does not entail *thinking outside the box*. You'll achieve recruiting excellence when you realize there is no box. You recruit—or fail to—with every ad you publish, everyone you meet, every day you work. Don't just pick one or two recruiting methods you like best; find ways to include as many sources and methods as you can handle. You will reach more candidates and gather a greater collection of talent and experience on your team.

Emphasize Active Recruiting, Not Passive Hiring

The most advanced version of recruiting is to attract candidates who are not looking for a job. Let me explain. Most recruiting methods are passive and only generate applicants who are actively seeking a job. These folks may be unemployed, recently fired, laid off, or nervous about losing their job soon. Please understand that there are many good reasons to seek a job, but also understand that this candidate pool includes a large number of people who do not have good reasons.

Your prime recruiting target is the person who has a job, is happy and successful in their job, and is not actively looking for a job. It is in this pool that you will find your best workers. You will find them by using some of the active methods discussed here.

Does this mean you should exclude talking with candidates who are actively seeking a new job? Of course not. As I said, many, probably most, have solid reasons for being on the market. You want to meet these people, but don't use passive recruiting methods exclusively. Sure, it's easier to sit back, run ads, and let the masses flock to you, but you will not draw the dynamic candidates you want unless you employ active recruiting methods.

Let's look at some of the diverse recruiting sources and methods. We'll offer some new ideas later, but right now let's examine some of the more traditional places to find employees.

TRADITIONAL CANDIDATE SOURCES

There are many traditional sources for finding candidates, such as newspaper ads, the Internet, and referrals. Much has been written about the use of these sources, and rehashing the plethora already on your bookshelf would not be beneficial. Let's use this opportunity to highlight some special uses of these media, as well as see how they apply to the entrepreneur's special needs.

The Classified Ad: The Historic Workhorse

The staple of recruiting for the past hundred years has been to run an ad in the paper. While it still has its advantages, classified usage has seen a steady decline for the past decade. It has been eclipsed by the Internet.

Despite this decline, newspaper classifieds still have their purpose and even offer some advantages to you. Here are some good situations for using newspaper classified ads:

- When you need to recruit a lot of workers at once; such as, for the opening of a new factory, warehouse, or restaurant.
- When recruiting lower-wage or hourly-paid positions. These applicants often turn to the newspaper classifieds as a first resort.
- When you have little lead-time. You can make a big impact quickly.

I recommend that you only advertise on Sundays. Besides the fact that the other days are rarely read, there is the added benefit of the Sunday paper's ability to attract people who are not "on the job market." Many people habitually browse the want ads while enjoying the Sunday paper. A well-written ad may spark interest from these readers.

Using Trade Journals

There is one use of classifieds not subject to many of the normal drawbacks. Advertising in your trade journal can be quite effective. First, you are being exposed to a large swatch of potential workers. Even people who have no intention of seeking a new job will routinely peruse ads in trade journals. They just want to keep up with what's out there. While they may not be looking for any new opportunity, your posting just might catch their interest. Also, regular ads in trade journals will enhance your name recognition. This will put you on their lists as a company to check out when the day comes that they are looking for a position. Here is an interesting bonus: according to research in performance patterns done by a psychologist at the University of Missouri, candidates who answered trade journal ads outperformed those attracted by other media. (Perhaps this is because there is less likelihood of a job mismatch when the candidate researches and selects a specific industry.)

Using "Blind Ads"

You may have an occasion in which you want to keep the fact that you are running a job search confidential. For instance, perhaps you are replacing an employee who doesn't know he is about to become a former employee. Maybe you are expanding your sales force but don't want to tip off the competition.

Avoid the temptation to run a blind ad that does not identify your company. Potential candidates who are currently employed will simply not risk applying for their own job. Use other methods, such as recruiters and referrals, if you need to conduct a confidential search.

The Internet: The New Workhorse?

The Internet job boards—complete with millions of active résumés from eager candidates—almost seems just too good to be true. Indeed, it is; the shear volume limits its usefulness. Job boards offer a tremendous volume of potential candidates, but often become overwhelming for both you and the candidate.

The Internet offers two ways to help you find people. First, is through posting an advertisement, much as you would in a newspaper. However, this medium has an advantage over paper: you have greater space to publish details about the job and skills you are looking for as well as plenty of room to sell your company to the potential candidate.

Perusing résumé postings is another way to find good candidates. Major job boards have millions of active résumés online. These sites have search engines that let you narrow down this small nation, classify résumés by geography, degrees, business disciplines, etc. This makes it a bit easier to examine a more manageable stack. The drawback to the Internet is volume. While this is a nice problem to have, every ad you post will receive a tidal wave of responses, most of them in no way related to the job you are offering. Searching through a million résumés, regardless of the excellent search engines, is often overwhelming. It is also impersonal. There just is no way to find that particular candidate who offers unique skills or who is a superior fit for your company's culture. I encourage you to take advantage of this medium but never consider it your primary tool. The Internet is simply too vast for building an entrepreneurial team.

Referrals

As every job seeker knows, networking is the best way to get the next job. As I explain to those I coach, 80 percent of available jobs are never posted, yet only 15 percent of job seekers seek these positions. The other 85 percent chase the 20 percent of jobs advertised on the Internet or held by recruiters. While networking offers great odds for the job seeker, it has the opposite effect on the company trying to fill a position. Despite these dismal statistics (from the employer's perspective), employers continue to use referrals to fill most positions.

There is a good reason for this: Referrals are an inexpensive method, costing nothing in most cases. It is quick, pain-free, and usually generates high-quality candidates. Let's look at how you can use different sources to make the most productive use of referrals.

Ask Your Employees

An employee referral program can be quite effective and inexpensive. Your current employees know your company and understand the jobs needed to be filled. Since they will work beside the person they refer, your employees will usually take care to recommend only people they would want linked to their name and reputation. Also, employees referred by other workers usually have a higher retention rate. This is because they have a built-in mentor whose personal reputation is invested in their success.

Should you offer a finder's fee? Do so as a courtesy or bonus if you wish, but my experience shows that paying a fee won't cause much of a difference in the employees' response. If you tell your team members what you need, they will let you know if they have any friends who qualify.

Use Your Suppliers

Your purveyors, suppliers, and even customers know the quality workers in your industry. They will often know of excellent candidates who can do the job and who may have even mentioned they are looking for an opportunity.

Post Openings Internally

Strive to have your company become known as a place where people can go to grow their careers. Internal hirings offer many advantages; you know the employees, their character, and their work ethic. They know you as well, so there is less concern about a job mismatch. Another benefit of internal postings: since everyone was given an opportunity to apply, morale will not suffer when you bring in a new guy.

Contact Your Trade Associations

Besides their familiarity with the people in the industry, they will also be aware of many candidates who have confidentially advised they are looking for a new position. Don't limit yourself to your specific association. For instance, if you are in the trucking industry and need an accountant, check with the accountants' groups, not the Teamsters.

Referrals offer you an excellent opportunity to recruit quality people inexpensively. Pay attention to its biggest drawback. Using referrals exclusively will severely limit your candidate pool. People you know will refer people they know and current employees will refer people from their own tight circle. Soon, you are dealing with a closed loop and you lose the advantage that casting a wide net will deliver. You will miss many great candidates if you use referrals as your only recruiting source.

Pirating

The best way to assure you hire someone who will fit the job and your company is to see them in action. Watch your competitors' employees at work and directly approach those that impress you. While this is normally a very simple process, here is a good example of pirating done on a highly organized scale:

Nucor is one of the country's largest steelmakers. They have learned that the best way to evaluate potential employees is to watch them work. Whenever they are at a construction site, managers observe plumbers, electricians, and other skilled workers. If they demonstrate the work habits Nucor prizes, the managers actively recruit them, convincing the workers to join their workforce. At Nucor, constructing a steel mill is often a stealthy job interview.

You can do the same thing, just on a smaller scale. Observe the people you come into contact with in both your business and personal life. Were you impressed by the woman who sold you your car? Did you get great service at a competitor's restaurant? Have you always been impressed by the friendliness of a certain cashier? Directly approach these people. Invite them for a cup of coffee, describe your opportunity, and develop their interest in joining your company.

Now this process may sound a bit unsophisticated. It may even feel a touch unethical. Realize that this process is *exactly* what an executive search firm does. Do it yourself and save a few thousand dollars.

Yes, poaching does have its disadvantages. If you are sloppy, you'll get a bad reputation. If you invade the same company more than once, you are subject to retaliation. If you really screw it up, you'll start a war. Poachers are vulnerable to being poached. If the company you target is a big vindictive one, they have the resources to wipe out your entire employee base. Done correctly and occasionally, poaching is a great way to cherry pick the best workers for your company. If used as a primary tool, as they say on medieval maps when they reached the unknown world, "Here there be dragons."

Community Programs and Government Agencies

You would be amazed at how many people and groups are begging to help you. They want to do it for free. What's the catch? I can't find one.

Your state operates an excellent employment center with an outstanding source of talent. These facilities prescreen, test, and evaluate candidates for proper job fit, as well as provide you with opportunities for job postings. Become familiar with the services available in your state. You will be excited by their professionalism, impressed with their offered services, and greeted as a hero. (You will also be delighted that few of your competitors exploit this source, so you will get more than your share of good candidates.)

There are also many community and church-based organizations dedicated to filling your positions. OK, they are actually dedicated to finding jobs for their members, but this is a case where the stars align. These programs vary in sophistication, ranging from simple résumé assistance to those rivaling the commercial outplacement firms. Contact these organizations and make them aware of your needs. They can be found through an Internet search or the Sunday newspaper's list of community organizations.

Educational Institutions

If you are trying to fill service positions or entry-level situations, take advantage of some of the excellent work-study programs offered at high schools. You can even partner with the school; the employees/students will not only work for a paycheck but also to earn a good grade. Their teacher will be a dedicated partner determined to ensure her students are successful, energetic workers.

If you need workers with vocational or technical skills, such as secretarial, electronic, mechanic, data entry, construction, or entry-level programming, contact nearby vocational and technical schools and junior colleges. Their job placement office will give you an enthusiastic welcome. They'll also assist you in interviewing, scheduling, and onboarding.

Colleges and universities are also enthusiastic partners to help you with all of your entry-level employment. Their placement offices are well organized and their staff is experienced with helping small businesses recruit. They will steer the right students to your interviews, be a source of temporary or seasonal professionals, and even set up internship programs that may lead to excellent employees post-graduation.

Build a relationship with nearby high schools, vo-tech schools, and colleges. Make them aware of your business, its plans, and future needs. They want to solve your need for qualified workers. Let them.

Walk-ins: The Mother of Recruiting

Many of us got our first job by impulsively responding to a sign in the shop window. This source is inexpensive, and applicants may be processed whenever vacancies occur. In addition, walk-ins provide an ongoing stream of candidates, which is vital in businesses with traditionally high turnover, such as retail and food service.

Walk-ins frequently become stellar employees quickly. This is because most walk-ins are already customers. They know your operations, enjoy the atmosphere, and understand what your customers want. This makes for a relatively quick onboarding process.

Don't think that the entry-level worker is the only person you can attract. Somewhere, right there in your zip code, could be an amazing executive who is fed up with the hour-long commute downtown. Then he visits the dentist across the hall, sees your sign on the door, and decides to stick his head in. Hey, it has happened.

Generating walk-in traffic also carries some disadvantages. Walk-ins show up randomly, often when you are busy and unable to deal with them. For instance, restaurants can not process applicants during heavy meal periods and managers can be irritated when they are interrupted at this time. I have known managers who eliminate applicants who inquire during the lunch period saying, "I'd never hire someone who applies during the lunch rush. Don't they realize I'm too busy to interview right now?"

Actually, no, they don't. You are often dealing with a young worker with no exposure to the job world that made an impromptu inquiry while eating lunch. Learn to adapt. You don't want this one to get away. Simply introduce yourself, thank her for inquiring, and make an appointment to speak with her at a more convenient time. (Or even better, buy her a cup of coffee, and ask her to wait a few minutes until the lunch line clears. Don't let her walk out the door and into someone else's.)

PROGRESSIVE OPPORTUNITIES

As an entrepreneur, using nontraditional methods is nothing new for you. No issue you deal with requires creative thinking more than combating the labor shortage. Ponder some of the ideas discussed in this section. While your competitors are fighting it out in the twentieth-century trenches, you could find some great additions to your staff.

Seek Those Others Ignore

Sometimes there are good reasons people are ignored, but more often this happens because of tradition, prejudices, or just because "nobody's

And, There's Always Mom

Nepotism has always been a staple for staffing new businesses. While I am sure you want to have the reputation for having enlightened, progressive human resource policies, don't ignore obvious solutions to difficult problems. Relatives can be a great source of staffing, at least on a temporary basis until you fully define the job you need to fill. That's because relatives have a vested interest in the success of your business. You know their abilities and their weaknesses, making it a bit easier to match them up with your needs.

As wonderful as all this sounds, also be aware of the disadvantages of hiring your mother. Hiring friends and relatives has its hazards. If handled poorly, it can create chaos in the work environment. Personal disputes can carry over into the office. Other employees may worry that a relative gets special treatment or be fearful that what they say may get back to the boss. Some relatives have a real issue taking orders from their child. (You run the risk of the rest of your team overhearing Mom saying, "Don't tell me how to do things. I used to change your diapers, you know!") The ultimate issue is: How could you fire Uncle Harry?

Here are a few tips to keep in mind when considering hiring relatives.

- Never hire a relative just because "they need a job." It's one of the movies' biggest business clichés: the incompetent son who only has a job because his father is the boss. Never get sucked into this form of patriarchal welfare.
- Sometimes spouses make excellent business partners and can work in incredible harmony but not often, especially if one spouse is the boss and the other is much lower on the totem pole. Good marriages are about equality and great conflict will occur when the spouse running the mailroom demands equality with the spouse running the company.
- Hold relatives to a higher standard than the other employees. Make sure the other employees see Junior earning his way up the ladder and that your brother doesn't get any extra privileges. When you hire relatives, let them know the extra burden expected of them.
- Make sure all rules apply to everyone equally. Morale will be destroyed if your brother-in-law takes ninety-minute lunches. Ensure that everyone is qualified for the job or they don't get hired. Everyone obeys the rules or they get fired. Ah, democracy!

ever done it that way." Entrepreneurs leap ahead of established competitors by executing fresh strategies. Use that method in searching for good employees. Here are some excellent underutilized pools:

Mentally Challenged

Fast food restaurants and grocery stores use this strategy successfully. They discovered that many so-called handicapped people have the skills and work ethic they need. As a group, they were friendly to the customer, always on time, and worked hard at jobs that others often felt were monotonous. Review your positions and see if some can be modified to use these splendid people.

Unqualified

You are asking, "After all the emphasis in Chapter 1 about listing qualifications, are you now advising I hire unqualified people?" Well, not exactly. Here is the strategy I am suggesting: Look for people with the character you need, and then train them on the job skills.

Use your hiring flexibility to hire potentially outstanding performers who lack critical skills, then provide the training for those skills. Hire a bookkeeper, and then pay her way through college to get a BS in accounting. Usually only minor technical courses are needed to get an otherwise ideal candidate up to speed on your particular computer applications. Because of its bureaucracy, MegaGlobal cannot be this flexible. You can.

Ex-Convicts

I once interviewed a candidate who listed *Inmate of the Year* on his résumé. You really have to admire his silver-lining approach to life! I'm serious here. There is indeed a talent pool available that includes men and women who have recently been released from prison. Many of the nonviolent offenders made mistakes, paid royally for these mistakes, and will spend the rest of their lives underachieving due to the stigma now attached to them. Realize that, every day, excellent drywallers, painters, plumbers, accountants, and engineers (the list is extensive) are released into a world that views them as lepers. This is a deep, untapped talent pool that offers you wonderful opportunities. (What about violent offenders? They can be a problem, especially if they explode on the job, leaving you open to charges of negligence. Check with a local employment attorney before going down this road.)

Obviously any relationship must be entered with your eyes wide open and an amazingly thorough system that ensures assimilation into your workforce. You will have to interview many ex-cons before you find a good match, but doing so is worth the effort because there are many highly-skilled, well-educated, and repentant people available who will perform brilliantly for the first person giving them a chance.

Buy Another Company

You would consider buying a competitor who had a great client base, excellent retail location, or a patent that would help grow your business, right? Well, people are your most important asset, so why not consider acquiring a competitor to pick up those critical assets?

There are some important pitfalls to avoid, of course. The culture fit must be right and you have to be assured that the employees will stay with you after the merger. Careful planning and open communication can overcome those issues.

Your Best Source of Employees

Here it is, hidden in the middle of the Chapter 2 of this book. Here is the best advice you will ever get on recruiting or teambuilding. *Hire retired workers.*

I play movie clips during my teambuilding seminars. A crowd favorite comes from *About Schmidt* with Jack Nicholson. The first part of the movie follows Jack as he eagerly begins retirement until the moment—about one month later—when he is bored beyond measurement. All those things he wanted to do, sleep late, travel, work around the house, spend more time with his wife and daughter just aren't as fulfilling as he dreamed they would be.

So one day, he visits his old office (which has been completely rearranged by the dweeb now sitting in his old chair) and slowly realizes that no one wants to take him up on his many offers of assistance. Forty years of experience enthusiastically offered and no one wants to grab it, even for free.

The workforce is potentially filled with Schmidtses: People with deep knowledge, experiences, and connections will appear on your doorstep with only a small nudge. Take advantage of this rich talent pool. Hire the retired worker. Let's look at some of the riches a Schmidt can bring to your table.

- *He is a motivated worker.* He is eager to fill his time, to be needed, to feel like he is contributing—to have purpose.
- *He is a bargain.* You don't have to train him or orient him with how the company does things. He only wants to work part-time (He retired from the full-time grind, right?), so he needs less money for providing you with the same core services of a full-timer. Because of his pension benefits, you don't even have to offer any of the fringes and other items that add 40 percent to the cost of all the other employees.
- *He can contribute some unique benefits.* For instance, he brings solid business relationships with your clients and customers. (Or, if he retired from a competitor, he brings *their* client relationships into your house.) He can also be a great mentor and trainer.
- *He offers staffing flexibility.* Let's use accountants as an example. For most of the year, he may like to work twenty-hour weeks. At tax-time, there is a good chance he will work full-time for a few weeks—a wonderful asset during a period when you'll need more people. The same principle works in the retail industry; his full-time presence is a blessing during the holiday shopping season.

This is a rich candidate pool that has not been tapped to its potential. Go out and tap it.

LONG-TERM PROSPECTING: CULTIVATING YOUR PIPELINE

The mechanics of a pipeline are quite amazing, actually. Pipelines work because of the synergy of capillary attraction. (You will be pleased to know this is the only time I use the word *synergy* in this book.) By attracting each other, which creates momentum, particles are drawn through the pipeline in a continuous stream. The pipeline stays full. If you put an air bubble into that pipeline, you break the capillary force that moves everything along. Break that continuity and you'll soon be sucking air. Scientists will tell you that it takes much more effort to get the whole thing moving again than it would have taken to maintain the pipeline.

Granted, I took a long route to make my point, but the point deserves the emphasis. As an entrepreneur, you are probably focused on today's needs, but fledgling businesses evolve into mature businesses as their management systems go from addressing immediate needs to planning for long-term needs. Go ahead and use the methods we just discussed to take care of that vacancy you are facing today, but use this section to create strategies to maintain the pipeline.

Be Involved with Your College

Build a close association with your alma mater. Readily offer support for the college, even volunteer to speak to different classes. Become close associates with the campus placement office and they will think of you first when talking to students who would make good matches for your company.

Adopt a School

If you run a garage, become heavily involved with technical high schools, and those offering mechanical studies. Do the same thing with food service. If you hire a lot of high school level employees or have entry-level positions requiring only a high school diploma, support a school with a specialized course of study.

Keep in Touch with Your Exes

Former employees know the job and know your company. You can bring them back into your business with minimal training, orientation, time, or expense. They offer no surprises; you know their capabilities and limitations. Hiring former employees takes the risk out of the process. Here's another reason to keep in touch with the exes: They can be a great source of referrals. They know the job and understand who is a good fit. Keeping on good terms with former employees develops a whole team of unofficial recruiters.

Attend Appropriate Career Fairs

Career fairs provide you with the opportunity to establish your image and project a stable, long-term presence. Regular displays at industry-specific career fairs, such as IT, telecommunications, engineering, and sales, help build your image in that industry. They are also excellent for establishing name recognition for the long-term.

Keep in Touch with Convention Contacts

You probably go to conventions to learn about advances in your industry or to set up sales contacts. Adopt an additional agenda and create a talent bank. Evaluate everyone you meet as a potential employee and add them to your talent bank. Make note of your conversations with these professionals, especially if they describe their career goals, desire to relocate to your area, or hint at any current dissatisfaction.

Keep Track of Your Competitors

Keep track of the activities of your competitor's key employees. Pounce on competitors' layoffs and downsizing. People who leave those corporations are well trained in your technical, managerial, and/or customer service skills, and can hit the ground running in your business.

Use Internship Programs

Internships can be developed into a great recruiting tool. A good internship program allows you to expose your company to an eager student. She learns about your organization, its goals, future plans, gets a feel for your culture, and learns a great deal about the job itself. A good internship will actually train and orient a potential worker as well as give you the chance to sell your company to her. That's a lot that can be accomplished during a short college semester. Here are some ways to build a great internship program:

- *Treat an intern the way you would a new full-time hire.* Give her the tools to do the job and the work space to do it. Thoroughly train her to do the job and let her know your expectations. Provide regular (and honest) feedback, just like you would a regular employee.
- *Provide meaningful work.* Interns seek challenging assignments and want to feel like they are contributing. Do not underestimate their capabilities; give them projects they can run with and take equity in. Never use an intern as a temporary patch to cover a labor shortage in areas below her expertise. Not only will she not consider working for you in the future, she'll dissuade her friends from considering you as well.
- *Pay interns well.* This may help you accept this concept: The best-paid intern is far cheaper than a low-paid conventional employee. A good paycheck (actually any paycheck) will give you a distinct advantage over other companies competing for the best interns.

- *Take a broad mentoring role with interns.* Most interns want to learn more than just the job skills themselves. They are also eager to learn about business in general. They crave career advice and hearing your perspectives. Develop a close mentoring relationship with your intern.

Interns provide you with an opportunity to recruit and develop some great future talent. Take advantage of this resource to cherry pick the candidate base at your local college.

NOW, REALLY GET AHEAD OF YOUR COMPETITORS

We've outlined a lot of strong sources for you to use for uncovering great candidates in a world that seems to be void of candidates. Use these and you can compete with any company out there. As an entrepreneur, you know that just pulling even with the competition will not satisfy you. You have got to be ahead of the pack. Develop a recruiting mindset.

Good team builders recruit when others don't. Of course, there are times you stop hiring but never stop the *recruiting*. Take advantage of economic slowdowns in the industry; these often provide opportunities to secure great talent that you might otherwise not be able to touch.

Never close the door on talent. The timing might be all wrong to bring aboard a great prospect right now, but another opportunity might present itself months or years down the road. Keep track of promising prospects, even if they make a move that seems to put them out of reach. They may move to another city, change career fields, or snag a high-salaried position with MegaGlobal, but someday their lives and needs could change. Maintain the relationship and await the new day.

As a responsible business owner, make certain that you maintain a good stock of office supplies, raw materials, and sales stock. You know that having a proper inventory is critical to the smooth operation of your company. Think of the applicant pool in the same way. If you truly believe that people are your most important asset, you will understand how important it is to keep a good inventory of talent. You can do that by maintaining a good applicant pool.

3

The Candidate Screening Process

For several crisp fall evenings every four years I'll nuke a bag of popcorn, ice down a tub of root beer, and plop down in my easy chair to watch the presidential debates. There they are standing before the American people, challenging each other on matters of great public discourse. Through this ritual, I have witnessed historic moments such as:

- Gerald Ford freeing Poland.
- Jimmy Carter consulting with daughter Amy about nuclear proliferation.
- Mike Dukakis coldly rejecting the death penalty for his wife's (theoretical) killer.
- Lloyd Bentsen telling Dan Quayle, "Senator, you're no Jack Kennedy."
- Ross Perot agreeing that he has no experience—at running up trillion-dollar deficits.
- Al Gore's sighing. Al Gore's lockbox. Al Gore sighing yet again.
- George W. Bush's "strategery," and hard work.

The presidential debates allow us to evaluate each candidate's grooming habits, as well as his ability to dress well and recite the clever one-liners written by his staff. Oh yes, the presidential debates are grand entertainment. Unfortunately, none of it has anything to do with one's ability to be a good president. In fact, "debating skills" ranks far down the list on the job description for president of the United States (perhaps, sixteenth, right after "paper clips").

Yet, as ineffective as debates are for picking a president, many people use them as their primary method for making their choice. Scary.

When it comes time to make a hiring decision, most employers base it on how brilliantly the candidate wrote the résumé, how spotlessly he dressed, and how cleverly he answered their nifty questions. Conventional interviewing—a question and answer session between candidate and employer—usually digresses with a nervous candidate reciting words he memorized from a book (*1000 Great Answers to Interview Questions!*) in response to an uncertain interviewer asking questions he got out of a book (*1000 Great Interview Questions!*).

When making a hiring decision, we put too much emphasis on an applicant's ability to *perform* at a job interview and too little emphasis on demonstrated indications that he is well suited to actually perform the job. Now this is just fine if we are looking for a professional interviewee, but how applicable is it for hiring a mechanic, programmer, dolphin trainer, or librarian? (Think I am exaggerating? Look at the advice given to students by an MBA program's recruiting guide: "Remember, the most qualified candidate does not always get the job. Many times, it's the person who interviews the best who gets the offer.")

You want to cut through the game and use a clear, no-nonsense system for selecting employees. Let me lay out my method for doing this. There will be no games, and no memorized answers to tricky questions. We'll just use three steps to identify the people with the best chance of thriving in your company. These steps are:

1. *The Résumé Review.* Your wide net will attract many candidates, and the resulting stack of résumés will initially appear overwhelming. This step will weed out the unqualified applicants, and identify those candidates holding the basic credentials you have determined are needed for the job.
2. *The Phone Screening.* You will then speak by phone to those who survive the résumé review, clarifying gaps in their résumé, drawing out their motivations, and getting a better understanding of how they will fit into your organization. By the end of your phone screen, you will have determined that the candidate is qualified for the job. You will also learn her motivations and start formulating a plan for recruiting her into your organization.
3. *The Face-to-Face Conversation.* Notice we call this is a conversation, not an interview. Also note that you have already determined that the person is qualified for the job before her shadow ever falls onto your doorstep. Since you have already confirmed that the candidate can do the job, this session (or more probably, "sessions") has but one purpose: to decide if the candidate will *blend* with your team.

Let's look at each step in turn.

STEP 1: THE RÉSUMÉ REVIEW—*ENSURING THE CANDIDATE IS VIABLE*

Managing the large number of résumés received for a typical job search can be an overwhelming task. However, I don't recommend the method Alex used. He looked at the thirteen-inch stack of résumés sitting on his assistant's desk. Over one thousand people applied for a sales position posted in the newspaper. "Here's what I want you to do," he explained to his assistant. "Save every tenth résumé and toss the rest of them in the garbage."

His assistant recoiled. "We can't do that," she reasoned. "We could be throwing away the best stockbroker in the state!"

"True," Alex replied. "But we don't need anyone around here with that kind of bad luck."

We must indeed whittle the stack down to a manageable group. I assure you we can do this by eliminating only the candidates who do not have

---

Focus: Setting the Right Tone

I'm sure you have recognized that my approach to recruiting varies considerably from the advice you see on most bookstore shelves. While most hiring and recruiting books treat the activity as a game, we will approach it as a business collaboration.

Here is what I mean: Let's look at recruiting the same way you would select a major vendor. We take great care in selecting this business partner, making sure the relationship is good for both parties. Like vendor selection, hiring a new employee is just as critical to your success. You should take the same care, courtesy, and respectfulness in initiating a relationship with your new employee that you do in establishing a partnership with the guy who supplies the paper clips.

Would you eliminate a vendor who holds a revolutionary new patent because you found some typos on his brochure? Would you eliminate a vendor who has a reputation for outstanding service because he was underdressed for your initial meeting? Even if you were qualified to do so, would you ask a vendor tricky pseudo-psychological questions attempting to probe into his latent state of mind? Of course not. Yet we often do these things when we explore our most critical business relationships. Recognize any of these?

- Joyce searches for typographical errors on the résumé. She believes a typo indicates a sloppy candidate.
- Erin minored in psychology and enjoys searching for the candidates' underlying issues. Her favorite question? "Is this glass of water half-empty or half-full?" (The correct answer to this question is: "It looks like you have about twice as much glass as you need there.")
- Roger begins every interview by saying, "Tell me about yourself," so he can see how well they can think on their feet.
- Kevin wants to see how a candidate handles pressure. He phrases his questions in a confrontational manner just to see the reaction.
- Sam has the applicant describe her strengths and then cleverly follows up by asking about her weaknesses.

Besides the fact that the candidate has already prepared memorized answers to them, these questions really tell you nothing about the candidate's ability to do your job or to get along with your existing team.

The recruiting process is not a game, sport, or battle. It is an attempt to build a business relationship that is far more critical than any vendor selection. Have a good, healthy, business conversation with a potential partner. Approach from that perspective to ensure recruiting success.

your basic credentials. Here is what we want to accomplish in this first step: Determine whether each applicant has the basic qualifications for the job and can be considered a viable candidate. Even though we are liberal in acceptance at this stage (if in doubt, keep them in the running), we should still be able to reduce the stack dramatically—possibly by as much as 90 percent!

How is that? It is a sad fact that many people pull out a shotgun with their Sunday newspaper. They blast their résumé to every job posted, even if there is no remote possibility they would be hired. Their logic? These folks come from the "it-doesn't-hurt-to-apply" school of job hunting. They have been advised that it never hurts to have your name out there, or "maybe they'll have some other job available." You can eliminate these inquiries without any further explanation or expenditure of perspiration.

So review the stack and reject those that seem to come from outer space. If you are looking for a programmer, eliminate those without any computer experience or education. Remove those who lack anywhere near the needed experience. (I'm *not* speaking of the candidate only having four years' experience when you have determined you need five; I am referring to someone who has been an assistant produce manager and you are looking for a VP of Marketing.) Do these seem obvious? Yes, they are. You will be shocked at how much of the stack will be eliminated at this stage.

Now the Hard Work Begins

The initial reduction is indeed easy and does eliminate most inquirers. Further examination requires more careful analysis. This task becomes less daunting if you remind yourself of the goal here: You are only trying to screen for the *obvious* issues, those that clearly remove the candidate from possible inclusion, and I do mean obvious. Give the candidate the benefit of the doubt if you are uncertain of a disjoint. Keep in mind that you will clarify the information and address all questions during phone screens.

Here are some do's and don'ts that will help you at this stage:

Don't reject your future loading dock foreman because his résumé isn't done well. Remember that the job seeker is not a professional candidate. Looking for a job is an infrequent activity that he is often learning on the fly. His résumé-writing skills have been learned from one of those gawd-awful books (with titles like *Job Winning Résumés!*). He has been taught that certain things should be said in certain ways (*use action verbs!*). Consequently, most résumés don't even reflect the actual personality of the candidate. Unless you are looking to hire a professional writer, discount the candidate's résumé-writing skills. Don't penalize an ugly résumé or give too much credit to a pretty one.

Do use your job description as a filter to identify whether the candidate meets the required and desired criteria. You will begin to relax your standards if you allow yourself to be distracted from these criteria you had given such careful consideration to establish. (Wow, look at this guy.

He doesn't have any sales experience, but he did work for the Big Time Glamorous Corporation—and they have a *great* sales department. Betcha he picked up a lot of neat ideas from them!)

Do give the applicant credit when he includes a well-thought-out cover letter. A good cover letter—matching her qualifications with your requirements—saves you a lot of time and shows she is serious about the job. Reward these people by taking some extra time to review their credentials.

Don't pay a lot of attention to the "Job Objective." With a few keystrokes, anyone can claim they are seeking the exact job you are offering. Don't get excited that you've found the ideal match when you read "from the time I was a ten-year-old boy, I dreamed of being the assistant sales manager of the third largest poultry company in Idaho."

Do remember that the purpose of screening résumés is to ensure that the applicant has all the *required* criteria, seems to have a *reasonable* match for the desired criteria, and brings some notable strengths to the table. Don't put more emphasis on the process than this, or you will prematurely reject some great candidates.

Make Note of Red Flags

What is a red flag? It is a résumé entry which gives you pause, something indicating a potential disjoint between this candidate and your job. Here are some examples:

- A history of short job tenure.
- Erratic career progression.
- Any regression in job title or responsibility.
- A non-chronological résumé format. (He might be hiding something.)
- Does not live in the city the job is based in.
- The "Objective" does not match the job you are looking to fill.

Here is something important to understand about red flags: Red flags are *questionable* items, not eliminations. If a résumé is riddled with flags, you may legitimately infer that the candidate is just too fuzzy to proceed, but do not let a couple of question marks cause you to reject a candidate. Instead, plan careful inquiry into these issues during the phone screen. In fact, highlight these and carefully scrutinize them, but don't lose a potentially good employee just because he made a format misjudgment.

Sometimes there really is a good explanation for having three jobs in eighteen months. Don't reject a candidate for this one flag. However, do make note of this issue, and all issues, knowing you will be able to fully pursue this on the telephone.

The résumé stack should be considerably shorter at the end of this step. Obvious disjoints have been eliminated, but the stack still contains some questionable candidates. Remember, we have been quite liberal in our acceptance at this point. We have done this for a simple reason—many fantastic employees are lousy résumé writers. Make note of your questions and concerns, list the gaps and uncertainties, and pass all of these folks on to the next step.

STEP 2: TELEPHONE SCREENING—*ENSURING THE CANDIDATE IS QUALIFIED*

The purpose of telephone screening is to establish credentials. You will explore the depth of those credentials, clarify questions you had about the résumé, and gauge the candidate's interest. By the end of the conversation, you only want to answer this question: "Is this candidate qualified to do this job?"

If the phone screen determines that the candidate does *not* have minimal credentials, he will be eliminated. The process ends there so you save yourself many hours of fruitless courting. However, if you verify that the candidate meets your requirements and does appear qualified, you will proceed with the process and have a face-to-face conversation. It is at this next step that you will clarify culture fit, his ability to work with your system, and identify other potential areas of contribution. However, that's later; right now, you just want to establish qualifications.

How do you certify those credentials? (Verifying credentials, at this stage, only means assuring a match between your needs and the candidate's *stated* qualifications. Right now we will assume he is telling the truth when he says he has an MBA. We will check references, verify education, and certify the claims at a later stage. Don't worry, we will be thorough about this; we just don't want to do it at this stage.) The best method is to thoroughly review two documents with the candidate: your job description and her résumé.

First, review the job description, go over each item and ask the candidate to tell you about how her background, experience, or education addresses the job requirement. Here are some questions that may be appropriate:

- This position requires relocation to Amarillo. Any issues with that?
- The job involves about 50 percent travel. How do you feel about that much travel?
- You would be our liaison with the ad agency. Have you had any experience doing this?
- We pride ourselves on being able to turn complainers into loyal customers. Have you had any experience doing this?

Just follow the job description you prepared and allow her to evaluate the connection. Then review the résumé, again ask for explanations for each entry. Just start at the top and review each entry in order. Ask obvious questions, such as:

- Your "objective" says you are looking for a sales management job. This job has a lot more sales to it than management. Tell me a little more about what you want from your next position.

- Why did you leave ABC Company and take the job at DEF Corporation?
- Why did you choose to major in anthropology? How will that help you in this job?
- It says here that you developed an in-store marketing display. Tell me about it.
- I'm concerned about the short amount of time you worked at the Really-Good Rivet Corporation. What was that all about?

You will find that the conversation will often branch into other related discussions. For instance, when she explains her work in pharmaceutical research, the conversation may turn toward government regulation of the industry. Give some leeway here. Hearing unprompted comments is just another way of evaluating credentials; you can find out if she actually knows her stuff or is just trying to bluff her way through.

These are rather mundane questions, aren't they? No snazzy inquiries, no clever tricks, no psychological analyses—just direct, simple inquiries. You ask about the obvious and get clarification on any area you are uncertain about. While not particularly sexy or exciting, this line of inquiry will lead you to verify the credentials of your candidates, and that is the complete objective of this step.

A bit of advice as you are evaluating the candidate's responses: *Recognize the limits of the telephone.* Eye contact, gestures, and posture are important to communication. Unless you are trying to hire a telephone salesperson, don't confuse the candidate's phone skills with her more applicable qualifications. At some point in the conversation you will recognize whether you are interested in further pursuing the candidate. It is time to plant the seeds for recruitment when this happens. Here are some things to cover:

Ask the Question

Say to the candidate: "If you were to come to work with my company, what would probably be the reason?" We'll explore the full value of this question in Chapter 12, but for now, understand this purpose. Her answer will tell you what her motivations are. You will learn what hierarchical stage she is at in her career and know what you need to emphasize when describing your organization. Ask this question and make careful note of the answer.

Find Out the Candidate's Income Range

Simply ask, "What was your total compensation last year?" We are not doing any negotiating right now; we just want to assure she is in the ballpark of what the job pays. If you are going to pay $70,000 and she is making a quarter of a million, there is simply no reason to go further. (Also note that if you talk to twenty candidates and they are making between $45,000–$60,000, you will need to adjust your plan to pay $30,000.)

Set Up the Face-to-Face Conversation

Do not delay. Make this decision before you hang up the telephone. Simply say, "Sharon, I'm impressed by what I've learned about you. You may be a great match for this position and I'd like to talk further. If you agree, let's set up a time to get together."

Send a Recruiting Package

In the old days, we demanded that the candidate do all the impressing and assumed that if we made an offer the candidate would automatically accept. Things have changed. Recruiting quality candidates now requires you to sell just as much as analyze. Let her know you are serious by delivering a package that contains information about your company. Include product brochures, organizational charts, newspaper clippings, your Web site address, coupons, a list of nearby stores, and information about your city (the chamber of commerce will be a big help with this). Send anything you have that will cast a favorable light on your company and the job. Don't wait until after you have made a final hiring decision to recruit; your recruiting begins *now*. Get her excited about your company before she walks through the door. If you decide not to hire her, the worst thing that can happen is you'll create a loyal customer and new member of your network.

STEP 3: FACE-TO-FACE CONVERSATIONS: *ENSURING THE CANDIDATE WILL THRIVE IN YOUR COMPANY*

I was teaching my second-grade Sunday school class a lesson about the wonderful creatures God created. To emphasize the variety of animals He placed on the earth, I began playing a small game. "What am I describing?" I asked. "He is gray with a white belly." They all looked at me blankly. "And has a bushy tail." Still no response, but many confused faces. "And he climbs in trees and eats acorns." Finally, Rachael, my prize student, ventured an answer. She sucked in her breath and courageously declared, "I know the answer is supposed to be Jesus, but it sure sounds like a squirrel to me."

The conventional job interview is not much more advanced than this dialogue. The boss will sit behind the desk and recite a list of questions. The candidate, who has studied for this day thoroughly, recites back the expected answers. Candidates are often prepped to the degree that they recall the expected answer while the boss is just a few words into the clever question or the interview might be original. It is currently vogue to ask magic bullet questions designed to evaluate how smart the person is, how they handle the unexpected, and how well she is able to express herself. All in one question! The trouble with magic bullet questions is that they quickly become clichéd questions and candidates prepare for them. Here is a sad example.

Michelle was seeking a job as a financial analyst in New York. At each round of interviews, at least one executive asked the identical question designed to analyze her analytical skills. In fact, the question was asked so often that she could anticipate it by the sly grin that crossed the interviewer's face just before he said, "How many degrees are there between the clock's hands if the clock reads 3:45?"

Months before, Michelle saw this question on a Web site so she had carefully rehearsed her answer. She would dramatically pause and almost whisper, "Wow. Now that's a tough one. Let me think for a minute." She would pause again, stare at the ceiling briefly and announce, "The answer is 180 degrees." Then she would quickly correct herself. "No, wait. That can't be right. The hour hand is already three-quarters of the way towards four. So, let's see, there are 30 degrees between each number, so the answer must be 157.5 degrees!"

Michelle felt no guilt for her performance. She recognized that the interviewers had already turned the process into a silly game when they all parroted the same magic bullet question. In fact, the game that had been created almost required that she should memorize answers to the questions she was most likely to be asked. She was just doing what seemed to be the way things were to be done, though she never understood how the process identified the best person for the job.

Although that particular question is a bit more sophisticated than most, conventional interviews generally follow this same pattern. The questions are known and the responses are memorized to a fault. Candidates know they will be asked to "tell me about yourself." They know to project their strengths (and give three examples) as well as sheepishly confess to easily forgivable faults. Accomplishments will be told in positive language (making use of action verbs). They come prepared with three brilliant questions to ask the interviewer, carefully designed to show that they have done a good job researching the company.

Forgive my cynicism. I am so frustrated seeing what should be an almost-sacred event reduced to the level of a party game. Not only has it become an ineffective ritual, it has been complicated to the point where you can no longer recognize the purpose of the interaction.

It doesn't have to be this way. It shouldn't be this way. The process should be a simple discussion between potential business partners. You are exploring a relationship and it should be done in the manner all potential relationships are explored. Not a formal Q&A, but a good, honest conversation between two adults.

So, this section is going to be much shorter than you expected. It certainly won't be composed of the advice every other book on "interviewing" provides. There are two reasons for this. First, you already have a bookcase full of books loaded with wonderfully tricky interview questions, so I don't need to duplicate this information. Second, I don't want you to conduct a traditional Q&A interview. In fact, you would make me a very happy man if you would just throw those other books away (or give them to your competitors).

If you prepared a good job description, conducted a thorough résumé review, and clarified credentials through the telephone screening, then you will have already determined that the candidate is qualified to do the job (and it is at this point that most selection processes end!). We all know that there is more to being a great employee than just having the ability to do the job. What remains is this: Will this candidate flourish in *your* company? We'll discover that by having a conversation.

What! No Questions?

Perhaps when I say you should "have a conversation," I am making it sound as though you should have a rambling, unstructured session with the potential employee. Relax, that's not where I am going with this. You should certainly have a plan for the conversation and direct the discussion. You must fully explore his personality, motivations, reasoning skills, and past performance. We must determine job match.

Yes, there will be some questions; all conversations include questions. They just won't be delivered in the horrible format previously discussed. Instead, your questions will be enveloped in what HR gurus call behavioral interviewing. This technique is based on the premise that past behavior predicts future behavior. (Pretty much like how credit is determined.)

A behavioral approach can be implanted into your conversation. For example, describe a current business problem. Then ask, "Have you ever dealt with something like this? Tell me what happened. What did you do about it?" Let the candidate draw the parallels, ask follow-up questions, explain his actions, and then play Monday morning quarterback for his own performance. Prepare a series of questions just like this, covering all aspects of the job you are discussing. You will be able to develop an accurate analysis of the candidate, one that provides a job-applicable understanding of how he would perform for your company.

Select a Productive Venue

Good conversations flourish in the right atmosphere. You learned this while dating; you can talk more easily during a walk in the park than sitting across a bare table. Let's look at some venues that are conducive to generating quality discussions. (Unless you are trying to hire a park ranger, I am not recommending a stroll through the forest.)

- *Facility tour.* Show the candidate your store, office, or restaurant. Have him meet the employees and observe his demeanor. Show the new products and let him analyze a product that is not selling well. Watch a video of recent TV commercials, let him read developing ad copy, or analyze the amazing success of a new mascot. Show him a ceiling leak in the warehouse and how the stockroom is arranged. You get the idea. Listen to his comments and war stories. A tour of your facilities will provide incredible insight into his understanding of the business, how he thinks, and how comfortable he will be working for your company.

- *Participate in a meeting.* Have him attend a meeting and encourage him to join in the discussion. This will give insight into his attitude, show how he interacts with others, and observe the quality of his questions. It will also give him a taste of the job and should—if he is a good match—motivate him to want the job. Besides, if nothing else, it's a good way to get some free advice.
- *Visit a competitor.* You can get similar insight into the candidate by taking him on a stroll through the competitor's showroom, shopping in his store, or dining in his restaurant.
- *Have dinner.* Breaking bread is the second most personal thing two people can do. A meal will quickly break down barriers and allow quick bonding. Don't do your entire meeting at the lunch table. Rather, use it to end the day or as a separate meeting.
- *Take a trip.* This is an advanced form of the facility tour. Again, this is not the venue for initial meetings, but as a wrap-up exercise for hiring executives. Taking a business trip together will answer a lot of questions—for both of you—about the potential for bonding as partners. You can observe personal traits such as timeliness, how he acts during mundane times, and energy level. He will show you his personal organizational skill, interpersonal skills, and social skills. The biggest benefit? It won't take long to determine how the two of you will relate on a day-to-day basis. If you two aren't going to be able to stand each other, it's a good idea to find out now. This will do it.

Making the Most of Your Time Together

In order to drive home the concept of a *conversation*, I have avoided giving you specific instructions for conducting the time you spend together. Additionally, I've avoided laying out formats, clever policies, and hiring gimmicks. Let me show you three things you may want to include in your discussions that might make it more productive.

Get Negative

So many interviews—oops, conversations—proceed as lovefests. It seems that everything clicks. You and she agree on everything. Her ideas are brilliant. She has successfully marketed products exactly like the one you are about to unveil. Heck, she's even left-handed, just like your favorite daughter!

I do not mean to mock the process. You may have indeed discovered a great employee but not a perfect employee. There are problems, irritants, and potential conflicts in every relationship. Just because you haven't found them does not mean that they are not there. They are and you've got to identify them before bringing this person on your payroll.

There's no fancy method to do this. Just explain that the job will not be all golden. Make certain you identify the company's weaknesses, issues, and possible stumblings. Explain the situations where you may not be the most wonderful person to work for and insist that she share similar insights to what she brings to the table.

Now, I don't want you to dwell on these negatives and turn a great conversation into a depressing one. Be certain you have exchanged insight into what each of you are like, just to assure both of you are getting a realistic understanding of what the relationship will be like. A wise philosopher—my Dad—once said you should never marry someone until you've seen them with the flu. Adjust the wording a bit and apply it to employment.

Reconfirm Her Motivation

The job is barely halfway done once you have decided that you want to hire her. Now, the even bigger challenge is to convince her to come work for you. We'll explore this step in the next two chapters, but for now I want you to gather as much information as you can about what she is seeking in a new job. We'll use this information to sell your offer on the things that interest her.

How do you do this? As mentioned earlier the best way is to *ask the question*. (I will repeat this throughout every section of this book.) We'll adjust the wording a bit to fit this situation and ask, "If you were to decide to come to work for my company, what would probably be the reason?"

Understand the importance of doing this. In order to sell any product you must address the customer's needs. Convincing someone to join your company is no different. Dedicate all needed time to knowing his or her employment needs.

Give a Five-Minute Warning

Here is an interesting bit of psychology: most people reserve their most important information until the last moments. Regardless of the time you have spent together, the candidate has reserved an issue to discuss with you when the "time is right." The right time never seems to happen, so it gets thrust in at the end. Forget the psychology and please don't analyze the candidate for doing this. You can identify this moment when he says, "Oh, by the way," "I almost forgot," or "One last thing." Listen carefully. You are about to learn something important.

What will you learn? It could be a confession. (I was once fired for embezzlement.) It may be a need. (My child has a medical condition and I must have specific health insurance to cover it.) It might even be something that sounds trite; be assured it is *not* insignificant if it is brought up at the end of the meeting.

Don't surprise the candidate by ending the discussion unexpectedly. You want to hear his oh-by-the-way statement, even if you have to drag it from him. Here is a good way to make this happen: Say, "We have about five more minutes, is there anything we should cover?" Never miss this opportunity to learn exactly what is on the candidate's mind. (By the way, you'll find this technique useful for *all* meetings, not just job discussions. Notice that salespeople, existing employees, stockholders, IRS investigators, and even your spouse will announce as dessert is served, "Oh, by the way." Know that you are about to find out the real reason they asked for the meeting.)

CALLING A SQUIRREL A SQUIRREL

"This is not at all what I expected from this chapter," you are saying. I'll bet you were looking for some really great interview questions as well as deep psychological insight into the subtleties of the answers. Despite my several explanations in this text, that may still be your perception of how to conduct a good interview. To that, I'll just turn Dr. Phil loose and let him ask, "So, how's that working for you?"

A simple procedure has morphed into a complex waltz. Let's take the interview back to where it once was and where it should be. Let's just talk, face to face, directly and honestly—just like we do in every other potential relationship in our lives.

4

Selecting Great Team Members

We are closing in on the finish line. After possibly months of searching, dozens of conversations, and unquantifiable pots of coffee, we are about to make an employment offer. What's left? We need to gather a bit more information about the candidate, verify his skills and credentials, and then make our decision.

VERIFICATION

Before we make our selection, we need to shine a bright spotlight on the final candidate. We'll verify the information on his résumé (commonly called "checking references") and collect new information about him by perhaps looking at his driving record, credit score, or other such investigations. Before doing this, we might want to test the candidate's compatibility with the job and your company.

Testing

The biggest reason for employee turnover is job mismatch. In other words, the employee was working in a job he was not well suited for. Sometimes this is caught early and the employee can shift gears, find his true calling, and get on with a successful career path. Unfortunately, this is rarely caught early and the person struggles for years, maybe a lifetime, in a niche that does not make good use of his talents or abilities.

Recognize this about job mismatch: Not only is it the number one reason for terminations, it is also the biggest reason for rotten, unfulfilling careers, and the top cause of unproductive employees. All these demons begin right at this point in the hiring process.

Both you and the employee are quite vulnerable during the recruiting process. The candidate may be seeking a job because he doesn't have one. He has a mortgage payment due in a few weeks and he will convince himself that *any* job is a great one. You may have needed to fill the job for quite some time and are anxious to hire someone. It is easy to convince yourself that this person—perhaps your only remaining candidate—is perfect. His desperation and your impatience can combine to make a costly mistake. Tread with care during this dangerous time. Let's look at some ways we can increase the odds that your future employee is well matched to your job and your company.

Assessments

Assessment testing is often a valid way to measure for job match. Many validated tests are available that can help you match the candidates skills to your job demands. What is it that these tests measure? Consider this scenario: You are looking for a parts manager for your auto supply store. In this job, he will look after an inventory of 40,000 parts, many of them looking similar or having similar sixteen-digit inventory numbers. You give your star candidate an assessment test that states he abhors detail, despises routine, and has a strong creative streak to boot.

Would this man be happy in that job? Of course not; he is as good a match to the job as the comedy team of Laurel and Costello. A good assessment identifies strong preferences and personality traits that often uncover blatant job mismatch.

A word of caution is in order. Written skill tests are indeed an excellent tool for assuring job match, but only if you use the right test. Some of the tests on the market are not designed to screen employees and should not be used to make hiring decisions. The Myers-Briggs Type indicator, probably the most famous of the assessment tests, is an outstanding tool for developing managers and for understanding personality differences among your team members, but it is not an effective tool for making hiring decisions. It just doesn't measure job-fit, nor does it predict job success, and should not be used for that purpose. (In fact, the publisher of Myers-Briggs states, "It is unethical and in many cases illegal to require job applicants to take the MBTI if the results will be used to screen out applicants.")

Skill Tests

Perhaps the best way to ensure that candidates can do the job is to have them perform the job. Skill tests are good methods for doing this, having the candidate demonstrate proficiencies in some aspect of the position. Skill tests or verifications have long been commonplace in the workplace and continue to play an important role in selection today.

AT&T was an early innovator in using skill assessment for white-collar jobs. Even in the 1950s, the candidate for a middle-management position would show how he would handle an in-basket exercise, prioritizing requests, phone calls, letters, and other tasks.

Skill testing can also include demonstrations. For instance, have potential salespeople explain how they would sell your latest product to Wal-Mart. Your potential press agent can write a press release under a tight deadline. Customer service representatives can show how they would deal with an irate customer.

These assessments and tests can be excellent tools for *helping* you make your selection. Put them in their proper perspective. Use the tests to verify information or enhance your understanding of the candidates, but never convert these tests to a scoring system that determines who you hire. These tests are tools, not a system in themselves.

Job Previews

Spending a day working with your company is an excellent way for both you and the candidate to discover how well the job fits. This is especially helpful for entry-level positions or jobs in radically different industries. For instance, spending a day trailing a server will quickly show the candidate whether the restaurant business is a desirable place for them to spend ten hours a day. Visiting sales prospects with your sales manager will help your potential sales representative decide if you share the same styles. Customer service representatives, chefs, teachers, and firefighters can all benefit from the opportunity to live in your environment for a day.

What if the job preview scares them off? This is not a problem. If the prospect is repulsed by your position in one short day, he most certainly won't stay on your payroll for long anyway. Think of all the money you will save in training costs. On the other hand, if there is a good match between the candidate and the job, the one-day preview will inspire and motivate him. This will make it so much easier to bring him on board as an employee, giving him an excellent start in his company orientation.

DIG DEEPER

You have now been presented with credentials and claims of glory, participated in excellent conversation, and been reassured by the candidate that he is a great fit for your organization. If it all checks out, you have made an excellent hire.

But there's the rub. Will it all check out? Is he who he claims to be? Are his accomplishments as golden as described? Is the résumé genuine? We must verify the accuracy of the information before using it to make our decision.

Employment Reference Checks

A long time ago in a faraway place, companies were quite cooperative in verifying employment information. Former bosses would provide candid critiques of their former employees. The personnel department would give details of dates, training classes, income, and earned bonuses.

Then, those companies found themselves on the bad end of lawsuits for slander, libel, and defamation of character—even if the information they provided was accurate. They were paying enormous judgments even for saying *positive* things about past employees. ("I was so proud of the way Fred bounced back from that marketing blunder and led the next big campaign.") These war stories have become so prevalent that now it is hard to separate the true horror stories from the urban legends. Today, companies are afraid to even acknowledge the person worked at their company for fear of becoming another case study for the lawyers that advertise on TV.

While this lack of cooperation is understandable, you need this information nonetheless. In fact, a person's past is the most important thing you need to know in order to make your hiring decision. How do we bridge this impasse?

Here is a simple, fast, and *legal* way to get around the company's reluctance to provide information: ask the reference to call you back. Call the reference at a time you are guaranteed to reach their voicemail. You'll say: "One of your former employees, Fred Schwartz, is being considered as a sales manager for our company. He listed your name as a reference. Please call me back if he was an outstanding employee." If Fred was an excellent employee, your call will be immediately returned. If not, the silence will be deafening.

Here are some other ways to get the most benefit from references:

- Ask each candidate, "What will your references tell me when I call them?" This serves two purposes. First, it lets them know that you really will be checking the references. Second, it gives them the opportunity to let you know their side of the story should there be any lingering issues. (An additional benefit: Since most companies are afraid to say *anything* negative, there is a good chance the only way you will find out about issues is from the candidate himself as he rushes to give his defense.)
- Talk to the candidate's former boss. The HR department prides itself on saying nothing while there is a good chance the former supervisor will be more forthcoming. Besides, the supervisor has firsthand experience and can provide a better analysis
- Network to get an evaluation of the candidate's performance. It's a small world; there is a good chance you know the candidate's former boss or someone who does. However, take great care as you do this. Don't speak with anyone who could tell his current company that their employee is out looking for a job. You could destroy your relationship with the candidate as well as ruin his career.

Other Background Checks

Your situation may require more information about the candidate, and there are several types of background checks you can consider for securing this information. However, when deciding on which investigations to do, you should be sure to select only those for job-related reasons. For instance, it makes a lot of sense to examine a candidate's driving record if he is to operate a company vehicle. It is just plain nosey if the information bears no relation to any job activities. Here is a roll call of some investigations businesses use most often.

Education

Education is the most often fudged résumé claim. It is surprising that candidates lie about this, since it is so simple to verify degrees claimed. All educational institutions will verify degrees and attendance. Most will do so by telephone—and they don't even require that you obtain the permission of the candidate. (Why are they so cooperative? Because they have a vested interest in ferreting out those who falsely claim to hold their degrees.)

Credit Reports

People won't manage your money better than they do their own. If this position involves handling a significant amount of cash or puts the employee in a tempting position from time to time, you may want to view the candidate's credit report. In addition to seeing how they are managing their money, these reports will also disclose liens and judgments.

There is a disadvantage to using these reports, however. And that is that they are often just plain wrong. A leading consumer magazine has shown that half (!) of the credit files they examined contained at least one major error. (A "major error" is considered one that could cause the rejection of a home or auto loan.) You do not want to compound this horrific outrage by rejecting a candidate based on an incorrect report. Before making any decision, always allow the candidate to view the report and make corrections.

Criminal Background Checks

Always perform criminal background checks on anyone in a position of trust, who handles significant cash, or who works around children. The process for having these checks may be complicated, so check with your state's labor department for exact guidelines.

Driving Records

Check these records before employing anyone who may drive on company business, regardless of whether he will be using a company vehicle or his own. Your company could face enormous damage if an employee with a bad record is involved in an accident, especially if it is disclosed that you did not check this before hiring him.

Drug Testing

Today's candidates not only understand your insistence on a drug-free environment, they actually consider this another good reason to work for your company. (In fact, eliminate any candidate who expresses a concern that you are "invading his privacy.") Being asked to take a drug screening does not insult good candidates, but the labs often do.

Take great care in choosing the laboratory you use for this screening. Many labs, particularly those with low prices and heavy volume, do the

---

Focus: A Good Marketer or a Downright Dirty Liar?

Challenger, Gray & Christmas, a prominent outplacement firm, closely examined 249,000 résumés and found that over half contained "discrepancies." Another study by ResumeDoctor.com found 40 percent had "serious discrepancies." And still other experts estimate that a third of job seekers shade the truth or flat-out lie on their résumés. What are the biggest areas for "discrepancies?" The top five are education, job title, compensation, reason for leaving the last job, and list of accomplishments.

A résumé is nothing more than an advertisement, a marketing tool. A little exaggeration can be expected and even accepted in any advertisement. Exaggeration can easily warp into fabrication, especially on a résumé.

While you can allow some puffery, you cannot overlook lying. So where is the line? Separate *opinion* from *fact*. Allow a candidate to take sole credit for leading a team, devising a great plan, or coming up with a great idea. Never tolerate a made-up degree or an exaggerated job title. A misstatement of *fact* on a résumé is a lie and the candidate must be eliminated from any further consideration.

Another note: Be stricter with résumé entries than you are with verbal comments. Realize that people can misinterpret questions or even bungle a spontaneous answer. A résumé is a thoroughly planned document that has been edited repeatedly. You can consider any errors in facts as outright lies.

---

bulk of their business in court-ordered follow-ups or police investigative work. They will often treat their clients as criminals. Good candidates have no problem being screened for drug use, but they expect to be treated with dignity and confidentiality.

You should personally go for testing at any lab you are considering. Not only will this ensure that your candidates will be treated professionally, but you can become familiar with the process your prize candidates are being asked to experience.

DECISION TIME

You could drag the selection process out for months, constantly adding to the bank of statistics, information, opinions, testing, and conversations. There comes a time when you should stop gathering information and reach a conclusion. It is time to decide.

Actually, no interviewing system would be needed if selection were only about getting the strongest, smartest, best candidates available. Cold statistics would determine who you hire. Those really aren't the only criteria, are they? Once you have screened candidates for their ability to do the job, get down to selecting the person who would best fit into your company. That is almost a completely subjective matter. So, no formulas here. No scoring system, either. From this point forward, it is all about your judgment. Let's look at some filters to use for making that judgment.

Avoid These Mistakes

The hiring process is filled with opportunities to stumble. Here are the "big three" mistakes employers make when evaluating candidates. Before making your final decision, ask yourself if your judgment is being manipulated because of any of these common fallacies in selection.

The Halo Effect

Perhaps the biggest mistake we make in evaluating people is letting one or two great answers or comments color our *total* impression of the candidate. For example, you might observe that the candidate showed great organizational skills and once designed a great sales campaign. Being impressed with these achievements, you then view all of the candidate's other actions as impressive. Don't analyze through a halo. Let each action or trait stand on its own.

You Make Up Your Mind the First Two Minutes

When I help people prepare for job interviews, I spend most of my time showing them how to make a great first impression. I remind them that most interviewers make their hiring decision in the first two minutes and the initial impression is far more critical than the hours that follow.

If a candidate arrives dressed to kill, gives a firm handshake, and compliments the golf trophy displayed in your office, you might be tempted to send him directly to personnel to start filling out his W-2. It also works in reverse: The gumchewer who fails to look you in the eye might have extraordinary skills beneath the rough exterior. Forgive some of the interviewing errors. Late? Dressed inappropriately? Mumbles? Sure, these are certainly strikes against them, but think twice before arbitrarily eliminating someone for initial mistakes. Yes, it is important that someone make a good first impression. Don't make your decision based on just that. (Another benefit of overcoming this mistake: Other employers, overwhelmed by the poor first impression, will reject some great candidates you can then hire.)

Grading on a Curve

When following a dud, mediocre candidates will look like superstars. Solid candidates will appear to be rather weak if they follow just after a skilled interviewee. Do not compare candidates to each other; compare each candidate to the job description you so carefully crafted in Chapter 1.

Take Time to Ponder

Go off to a quiet spot and ask yourself some questions about the candidates. Look beyond their résumés and statistics. Instead, focus on the impressions each candidates has conveyed and the potential character of your work relationship with him. Ask yourself questions such as these:

- How well does she fit the job description?
- How did her background checks line up with her résumé?
- Did the other people who spoke with her get the same impressions I did?
- Do I trust her?
- Is she excited about this job?
- How will she interact with the rest of my team?
- Does she have strengths in the areas I most need from him?
- Will she represent me well?
- Do we communicate honestly and openly?
- Can she grow and assume expanded responsibilities if the company were to grow twice as big?

You will want to add more questions to the list, but this should get you started. The point is to find the time and patience to really examine the person and quietly discover the depth of the potential relationship.

After All the Facts Are In

You're going to love this next bit of advice. Once you have gone through the process, spoken, verified, and examined, it gets down to listening to what your gut is telling you.

If your gut is telling you to hire a person, it is almost certainly right. Your basic business instincts are a legitimate decision-making mechanism.

Before you throw your hands in the air and wonder why I didn't tell you to follow your gut before making you absorb fifty pages of selection technique, let's clarify this. The reason your instincts work at this stage is because you have educated yourself about the job and fully explored the candidates. Your gut is really an amazing computer that will churn all this information, combine it with your business knowledge and experience, and then sift it through your inherited good judgment. The "gut feeling" you get is the end product of all this processed information. Ergo, your gut is a great decision maker *only* after you follow the processes described in Chapters 1–4. This is where recruiting morphs from being a science into an art— highly trained art, but art nonetheless.

But What If You Eliminate Everyone?

It happens. You begin with a thirteen-inch stack of résumés and one by one they bite the dust. What do you do if you go through this entire process and have no one left to hire? You may be tempted to pick the best of the sad lot and be done with it. Overcome this temptation. If your job description was realistic and appropriate when you began this process, stick with it. Don't lower your standards or settle for mediocrity.

Start the process over, but this time use different sourcing methods. If during the first time you used only passive methods, such as the Internet or classified advertisements, expand your pool by seeking referrals or by pirating. If you thoroughly evaluate your activities and honestly believe you have done the best you can do, then you should consider employing an executive search firm. Yes, this is expensive, but the cost does not approach the money you will lose by placing a bad employee in the empty position.

Barbara had reached the end of an exhausting selection process and uncovered two outstanding candidates. The finalists were amazingly similar as well as equally talented. Reviewing their qualifications, experience, and credentials did not solve her quandary; these were also amazingly equal. To really exacerbate the issue: She honestly liked them equally.

She decided to settle the matter by giving them a test about the company's products. As you probably guessed, the finalists once again scored the same. Not only that, they missed only one question—and it was the same question! Despite this, Barbara was able to immediately make her selection. She called the losing candidate and told him of her decision.

He was shocked. "How could you make a decision based on that?" he asked. "How could one wrong answer be better than another wrong answer?"

"It's like this," Barbara explained. "For question #67, the other guy wrote, *I don't know*. And you wrote, *Neither do I*."

Sometimes, despite our efforts to use careful scientific analysis, it all comes down to using common sense and listening to our gut. The selection process is often like that. After all you have been through, you might feel that the hard work is complete. Sorry, it has just begun. Now we need to convince the candidate to become an employee, then assimilate her into the team.

5

Bringing Them Onboard

Here is a humbling thought: Once you have decided whom to hire, the job is perhaps halfway done. What remains? You must convince this star employee-to-be to accept your offer. Fifty percent may be optimistic; as time passes and the labor pool shrinks further, those odds might fall to 33 percent.

So, think of all the effort you have given to this point. Then double it or triple it. That is now what you have to look forward to. Why is this? This is so because there are still several people and situations conspiring against you. Consider these:

- Another company makes a "better" offer.
- You do a lousy job of presenting your offer.
- The candidate's spouse vetoes the move.
- The current employer makes a great counteroffer.

Now that I have your attention (and have probably generated a new bout of depression), here's the good news: While 91.6 percent of your competitors are bumbling their way through this process, you will learn a quick and effective method to capture these prized candidates. (Coincidentally, mathematicians will verify that 91.6 percent of all statistics are made up on the spot.) Let's start with preparing the offer.

WHAT'S THE SALARY OFFER?

Here is a snippet from the salary negotiations for my first job. When asked what kind of income I was looking for, I replied, "I certainly want to be paid what I am worth." His reply? "Can't do that. Minimum wage laws get in the way."

While there is much more to making an offer than salary, we would be naïve if we didn't acknowledge the incredible significance it plays in influencing the candidate's decision. So, how do you determine the right salary offer? Here are some good approaches:

- Look through your notes during the phone screenings. You asked each candidate what his or her salary was last year. Use this to establish a range. (For you analytical-types, rank the candidates and then put their salaries on a graph. Perhaps you will find a correlation, but you are more apt to see that compensation is not good science.)

- Certainly pay close attention to comments the candidate made during the selection process, particularly his current salary. If you actively recruited the candidate, that is, you approached him when he wasn't looking for a new job, then you must offer *at least* 20 percent above what he is making now. On the other hand, if the employee approached you or is currently unemployed, a modest 5 percent increase may be an adequate incentive.
- Don't even consider taking advantage of the fact that he is currently unemployed and may even be desperate. Yes, he'll accept your low offer, but will resent you a few months down the road. The cliché penny-wise and pound-foolish comes to mind here.
- Do consider the dramatic variation in cost of living in the USA. Your offer may need to be adjusted if the employee is to be relocated. For instance, a person moving from Birmingham to San Francisco would require a 44 percent increase just to break even. No, it doesn't work that way going the other direction. While mathematically someone transferring from California to Alabama would break even with a 31 percent pay cut, no candidate would even accept such an offer. However, you can use this information to explain why your salary offer is not as big of an increase as it normally would.

While the salary offer is certainly important in hiring your candidate, don't agonize over this. As a headhunter, I never had a deal fall apart due to salary at this stage in the process. This is probably because any large gaps are identified early in the recruiting process. You have a pretty solid idea of his expectations and have chosen to go forward.

After all this information-gathering and analysis, my advice for setting salary is the same as that I gave for selection: use your gut. If all the other aspects of the offer are appealing, the salary issue will fall into place. If this employee truly meets your needs, it is appropriate for you to be the one to bridge any remaining gap.

PAINT THE PICTURE

Consider this experience: Two companies made identical bids for painting my house. The first company gave this proposal:

Two-story house painted, complete services, $3,400.

That was reasonable, especially since it came from an old, established company several friends recommended. Then, I opened the second bid. It read:

Executive Painting Package for the Tanner Family Home

- Cover all nearby shrubbery and landscaping to assure there is no paint or chemical damage.
- Restore any loose nails or boards.

Focus: Another Take on Compensation

I have always advised companies that people will not leave a job they like for a lateral salary or even a pay cut. My thoughts have evolved over the past few years and I need to share with you an exception to this previously concrete compensation rule. As we will explore in Chapter 14, sometimes people reach a point in life where they seek benefits from a job other than money.

I have a client that is a good example of this. Operating a large chain of for-profit Christian radio stations, the client has a deep need for experienced advertising salespeople. Even though their budget allows them to pay only about 75 percent of what other radio stations pay, my client attracts some of the best people in their markets. They do this by stressing the other things they offer, such as a positive atmosphere, deep culture, and the fulfillment that comes from the product they sell. They can attract mature (that is, experienced) talent who—having their children out of the home, the house paid off, or whatever—can now afford to take a lower income in exchange for working for a company they believe in.

While this does not work for everyone (in fact, it doesn't work for most companies), you may be able to offer some intangibles that offset some of the salary. Most nonprofits offer the feeling of accomplishing something; your candidate may be willing to take a pay cut to be on the ground floor of your exciting enterprise. Maybe your location is so much closer to home that the candidate will be willing to take a bit less in exchange for having many more hours with the family. Perhaps he travels four days a week with his current company and will only have to travel two days a week working for you.

While it is usually true that you cannot attract top talent without offering a significant pay increase, don't write off the possibility. You may be able to snag a superstar by offering him something he wants more than money.

- Caulk all gaps and chipped areas.
- Perform full deluxe pressure wash to remove all mold, chips, and loose paint.
- Apply full prime coat to properly seal paint to wood.
- Apply two coats of premium semigloss latex paint, your choice of over 8,000 colors.
- Apply same premium paint to all trim, stairways, and windowsills.
- Fully clean paint from all windows.
- Completely inspect all surfaces and repaint any areas missed or not done to the highest standards.
- Remove all equipment and perform complete cleanup of the work area.

Total cost, including labor, materials, and taxes: $3,400

Understand that the scope of services and the quality of workmanship for these two companies were identical. Which one do you think I chose?

It was his presentation during the screening process that convinced you to hire the candidate. Now it is your turn to do the convincing. As my marketing friends will declare, *how* you present the offer is almost as important as the offer itself. Let's look at an outline of a good offer presentation.

Subject 1: Money

Go ahead and declare the salary offer, along with describing any bonuses, or other cash considerations. Why do this on the front end? Why not discuss the other reasons to join the company and then zap them with the cash? Because the candidate will not be paying any attention to you until he hears the salary. If you delay the salary offer until the end, he won't hear about all the wonderful benefits, and he will think that the salary offer is going to be a low one. Get this out of the way up front.

Subject 2: The Financial Benefits

Explain the benefit package in detail. This is a critical issue for most employees, so he will be impressed with the long list of compensation benefits he will receive on top of the salary offer. This will not only add to the reasons he should want to work with you, but its placement here will also enhance the value of the salary offer. Outline these benefits:

- Health insurance
- Credit union membership
- Travel benefits
- Vacation
- Company auto
- Retirement benefits
- Bonus program
- Life insurance
- Merchant discounts
- Educational assistance
- Sick pay, bereavement pay
- Savings and stock plans
- Equity

While you describe these benefits, it is important that you also tell him their dollar value. For example, having a company car is easily worth $10,000. Health insurance costs a family at least $8,000 per year when purchased in the private sector. What is the cost of that MBA you are willing to pay for? Add these numbers up and the candidate will be amazed (as will you) at the value of these benefits others take for granted.

Incidentally, include in your calculations the dollar value of *all* the benefits, even if you don't personally pay for them. For example, credit union members can get car loans several percentage points lower than they would see at their bank. While you aren't directly making this loan, you are providing the vehicle for the employee to save several hundred dollars a year. It doesn't matter to the employee whether you write the check; what's important is that if he works for your company he will have an extra three or four hundred dollars a year in his pocket. Take credit for this.

Subject 3: Other Benefits

We are speaking of more than the financial benefits. Very often, it is a nonfinancial benefit that entices someone to take a new job. Here are some good examples:

- A more prestigious title.
- Your office is closer to his home than his current job; commuting time could provide him with an extra five hours per week with his family.
- An exciting challenge.
- Greater responsibility.
- More independence.
- Nicer co-workers.
- The opportunity to learn more about other disciplines.
- The opportunity to participate in broader decisions beyond his specific niche.
- A more formal work atmosphere.
- A less formal work atmosphere.
- The chance to make an impact.
- The chance to be appreciated.

Here is an important point: these nonfinancial benefits are often the deciding factor for people accepting a new job, particularly for the mature worker or for senior-level positions.

CLOSE THE DEAL

Throughout this book I have emphasized that you should regularly ask the question. This question has incredible power in retaining your team, but here is where it serves you in recruiting. You will use the information you have gathered to close the sale. Conclude your presentation by saying: "Oscar, throughout our conversations these past few weeks you have repeatedly told me that you want three things in your next job: a positive culture, a family-friendly schedule, and an absence of corporate politics. We will meet those needs. Will you join us?"

If you are competing with another company, this comment could be what tips the decision in your favor. Realize that the other guys are probably focusing only on salary. They give little attention to the benefit package and will completely ignore the key needs he has told you about. You will gain a tremendous negotiation advantage by addressing the very things the candidate lists when asked the question, "If you were to come work for my company, what would probably be the reason?"

There will be some conversation following this proposal. He may ask for further clarification about the benefits, mention some other special need, or feel the obligation to negotiate salary. Don't be offended by his need to negotiate. Candidates are coached to never accept the first offer. (There is always another envelope in the desk drawer, he is told.) Actually, you may be legitimately surprised if he doesn't try to negotiate.

Don't let the salary discussion linger. Wrap it up on the spot. If postponed, small gaps become canyons, often unbridgeable. Decide before your meeting how much you will add to your offer and respond immediately. Again, other issues may be discussed, but don't be bothered by this or think the candidate is trying to nitpick you. This is an important decision and he is just trying to understand the details.

The discussion will probably conclude with the candidate asking to have a few days "to discuss it with my spouse." This is a reasonable request. Agree on a date for you to receive an answer (never more than a week). Assure him that you would be delighted to answer any questions or talk further in the meantime.

IF HE SAYS NO

You have just made your "pitch" to a prospect to buy your new perpetual motion machine. The prospect says no. Do you pack up your sample case and politely say, "Have a nice day!" as you sulk to your car? Of course not. You use that *no* as an opportunity to discover the prospect's objection, then make another proposal. It works the same way if your candidate declines your offer. A client recounts his experience in dealing with a candidate's rejection:

> A great candidate I had been recruiting for months declined my offer. I called him and said, "You gave the wrong answer." At dinner that evening (this time with his wife in attendance), I identified the real issue that was holding him back. As it turned out, his wife wanted the family to take a long-planned European vacation scheduled to begin two weeks after the starting date I had insisted on. I quickly agreed to a new date and even threw in a modest signing bonus to help with some of the vacation expenses. He agreed on the spot to take my offer.

(An observation about this flexibility: it was logical to bend on this issue since the process of hiring someone else would take so much time that there was no way the start date could be met anyway. The $500 signing bonus was a tiny fraction of what it would have cost to begin the search anew.)

The discussion does not end when the candidate says no. If this is someone you want in your organization, then reopen discussions, and ferret out the real reason for his rejection. Sometimes, just the simple act of trying again will be enough to bring him on board.

LOCK IN THE DECISION

Three days pass, your phone rings, and you are greeted by those three little words everyone wants to hear: "I'll take it!" Has the process finally ended? I'm afraid not. Many employees change their minds between acceptance and going on the payroll. Here are some of the reasons this happens:

- The current employer makes a counteroffer.
- The kids are upset at having to change high schools.
- The candidate gets cold feet or has second thoughts.
- The candidate has been talking to more than one company and they made him a better offer the day after he accepted yours.

Actually, with all these demons fighting you, you may start to believe that it is impossible to get anyone on your payroll. Relax. These problems can be managed successfully once they are identified. Just understand this: there is a strong chance you will lose him if you ignore reality between the time the candidate accepts and the day he is supposed to report. You can reduce that possibility significantly if you execute a good transition. Here's how.

Immediately Warm His Feet

Have your new employee immediately come to the office and fill out all the employment paperwork. Signing his name to a stack of forms will mentally lock in the finality of his decision, preempt his developing cold feet, and help cement the relationship. Even though most of these forms are routine, such as the W-4, processing these papers may have the moral impact of a contract. Because he has "signed on the dotted line," he will subconsciously drop any second thoughts or lingering doubts. (Consider it an omen if he hesitates in taking this step. He may have not made up his mind or could possibly have another offer about to come in.)

Preempt the Counteroffer

There is an excellent possibility that his employer will be shocked when your prize catch turns in his two-week notice. If your new hire is as good as you think he is, you can probably expect this company to work hard to keep him on their payroll. Companies often respond to resignations with counteroffers. You need to be prepared for this and preempt its impact before it happens. Meet with your new hire and say:

Let me tell you what will probably happen when you give your notice. There is a good chance your boss will be shocked and want to do anything he can to keep you. He may promise you more money, consider you for a promotion, or shower you with superlatives about the incredible future you have with the company. All this will be terribly seductive. When it happens, you need to ask yourself, "If I am so important to them, why did I have to quit to be noticed?"

It never pays to accept a counteroffer. Every time I have seen someone accept a counteroffer they have left the company within a year. And you can see why. After a few weeks, when all the excitement has calmed down, your boss will begin thinking that you manipulated him. He will figure that since he had to fight to keep you, you should be doing a better job. Since every company has a grapevine, your peers will resent the way you got a big raise.

There are a lot of possible scenarios, but the bottom line is that things will change for the worse. Believe me on this, counteroffers never work out in the long run. When you resign, emphasize that you have given the decision a great deal of thought and your decision is final.

Does this sound like overkill? It is not. Almost certainly his company will make an effort to keep him. This attempt will be seductive and flattering; your preparation will make the difference.

Involve the Spouse

No one has more influence on the employee than his or her spouse does. If not done already, immediately make contact with the spouse. Sending flowers or other gifts makes an excellent icebreaker, but don't stop there. Invite the spouse to the paperwork meeting, show her around the office, and discuss her spouse's new job. Ask her if she has any questions, address concerns, needs, comments, or anything on her mind to discuss. Address all these questions with the three of you sitting around the table. Introduce her to her very own company mentor—the spouse of another employee who will be her direct contact throughout the onboarding process. Provide assurances to the spouse that she will be included in the orientation process, especially while discussing employee benefits and insurance.

We will have a more detailed discussion about involving the spouse in the next section, onboarding. For now, understand the importance of making that *initial* contact.

It Starts Now

The onboarding process starts now. Treat the candidate as an employee from the moment he says yes. Here are some more ways you can do that.

- Immediately assign and deliver his company car.
- Issue his laptop along with his e-mail address, passwords, and the company's e-mail directory. Have a welcoming message already on his e-mail inbox.
- Issue his company identification card, corporate credit card, uniforms, tools, etc.
- Allow them access to corporate web pages so they can get ahead of the learning curve before actually starting in their new job.
- Immediately involve the employee in all social activities. Have a softball team? Weekly lunches? Is the company having an outing, field trip, or weekend barbecue? Make sure he's included.
- Assign a mentor to assist during the transition. Have her contact the new employee before the start date. She can prearrange meetings with new peers, provide a full facility tour, etc.

- Give him a telephone directory updated with his name in it.
- Find out who he would like to meet during his first week. Schedule the meetings before they start.
- Deliver new business cards to his home.

Don't overlook the opportunities available during the gap between his accepting your offer and actually being placed on your payroll. It could mean the difference between having an employee starting work excited and comfortable or not starting work at all.

ONBOARDING

This is a true story:

Josh was squished by an airport courtesy van and found himself meeting with Eternity's Gatekeeper. "Here's how it works," EG explained. "You get to spend a day here and a day down there. Look around, talk to the residents, and ask all the questions you want. Then let me know where you want to spend eternity."

Josh was grateful for this right to choose. He toured the upper venue and was impressed with the peace and quiet, golden streets, as well as the beautiful scenery and unlimited refills of caffeine-free Diet Coke. *Not a bad place to spend eternity*, he thought.

The next day, he toured the other option and was quite surprised with what he found. There was a lot of exciting activity. He liked the party atmosphere, the tasteful pictures on the walls (Elvis on velvet was his favorite, of course), and the nonstop poker games. He enjoyed conversations with famous politicians and marketing executives, as well as debates with the many lawyers and umpires who had retired there.

The gatekeeper was not surprised with his decision. Josh giggled as he hopped into the hand basket and was quickly whisked away to his new home.

He was shocked when the doors opened and he viewed a landscape of burning embers, parched, cracked earth, and filthy residents wailing in pain as they received never-ending root canals while reading IRS manuals. Flames kissed their toes and the stench of sushi was everywhere. Even the Elvis picture was gone. "What's going on?" he asked a nearby supervisor. "Where are the poker games? The delicious refreshments? The dancing girls? The sparkling conversations?"

"You need to understand something," the supervisor explained. "Things have changed. Yesterday you were a recruit. Today you are an employee."

OK, perhaps that is not a true story, but at the end of their first day, many new employees can easily relate to it. They have just attended the orientation from hell and second thoughts are quickly forming. "How was your first day at the office?" her husband will ask. "Oh, it was wonderful! They let me fill out dozens of forms, told me the rules, all the ways I could be fired, and then let me watch a video about the evils of sexual harass-ment. Yes-sir-ee, I'm going to love working there!"

Nothing kills all the positive momentum you have built quicker than a lousy first day on the job. The orientation has a strong impact on the employee's long-term success. That initial exposure to your company sets the tone of the future relationship. She will establish her co-worker relation-ships, decide on her role in the company, bond with her new boss, and develop her image of the job, your company, and you. There is an exact parallel between the impressions you formed within the first few minutes of meeting the candidate and the impressions she forms on the first day on the job. Yes, the onboarding process is that important.

A well-thought out orientation program can help new hires feel at home right away and also make it possible for them to get started on the right foot and quickly become productive. Research shows that improving orien-tation can increase retention rates by as much as 25 percent, while initial frustration slows time for productivity, increases error rates, and can rob new employees of their enthusiasm.

Let's look at an onboarding process that serves to promote goodwill instead of terrifying the new employee.

Commit to Full Training

Here is a mistake I witness too often: A position has been left unfilled for weeks or maybe even months. Finally—finally!—someone is hired. After a brief greeting, and possibly a great orientation, the new superstar is tossed right into the job without proper training or development. Managers are especially vulnerable here, especially if they come from a similar system. For example, a Wendy's manager hired for McDonald's, a New York cop transferring to Omaha, or a widget foremen now supervising the creation of wadgits. The logic is that concepts are similar (though they really aren't); he's a sharp fellow and will figure it out.

This approach guarantees failure. You have invested significant cash, sweat, and effort in landing this outstanding employee. Commit, *right now*, to give him complete training. Invest the time required for him to hit the road fully prepared and confident in his abilities.

Prepare Your Organization

You are courting disaster if your existing team first hears about the new hire—or even first learns of the possibility of a new team member—the day that he walks through the door. There may be many good reasons for you to have conducted the search quietly, but once a decision has been made you should immediately inform your team of the new person that will be joining them. Pay special attention to anyone already in your organization that would have wanted this new job. Deal with this issue before your new hire reports to work or else this prized recruit will suffer the daggers thrown by the jealous co-worker.

However, if you are like most entrepreneurs you did not fill this new position until your existing employees started begging for relief. They would have been excited if you hired a two-headed Martian, if for no other reason than because they are exhausted and welcome the manpower. While this situation provides you with a receptive audience, don't let their good attitude prevent you from keeping them fully informed. Even if they have participated in his "interviews," bring everyone up to date on his résumé and background, and review the job description for his position.

Review with your employees the importance of issuing a friendly welcome as well as their role in his assimilation with the company. Ask one peer to serve as a one-person welcoming committee and help bridge the new employee's introduction to the company culture and routine.

Focus on the Family

Earlier I mentioned the benefits of including the spouse in the whole process. This becomes absolutely critical during the employee's assimilation into your company.

No matter how wonderful their relationship, the employee usually fails to pass information to the spouse that is important. For instance, details about the health insurance, often critical to the spouse, is given short study by the employee. Other facts about benefits, extent of travel, even what the new city will be like, are lost in all the jumble of information, and rarely passed along to the rest of the family. This causes great frustration for the family and only makes the employee's assimilation more difficult. Anticipate these anxieties and help alleviate them. Bring the employee's family into the process as much as possible. Here are some ways to do that:

Communicate the Benefits

Have the spouse attend all meetings describing benefits, particularly discussions of the health insurance. In fact, have the spouse meet with the insurance company's representative and be the one to make any selections of benefits or plans.

Assign a Spouse Mentor

If possible, have the spouse of an established employee become an ambassador for the new employee's spouse. Spouses are often uncomfortable contacting the employer, but will eagerly have an informal chat with a peer to answer a few quick questions.

Deal with Relocation

Be especially attentive if relocation is involved. Relocation is a major issue in a family's life and you can be assured that your new employee has very little time to give his family the support needed through the process. Contract with a relocation expert to consult with the family and provide detailed assistance. Professional moving companies will have a staff member who can offer excellent services; this is usually included in the price of the move itself.

Also, be aware of the tremendous stress relocation places on children. Moving to a new school, especially if it is a high school, is a life crisis for a teenager. Leaving their friends is also and could combine to create an unpleasant domestic situation during your new hire's first few months. Why should you care? Because domestic disharmony often causes your prize employee to change her mind, quit her new job, and return to her old life and city.

Help with the Move

If the employee is being relocated, do more than just pick up the tab. Put the family in contact with an excellent real estate agent. Have the chamber of commerce provide them with all the charming details about the new city. Arrange for the new high school to assign a student to be a new mentor for the kids. Do everything you can to address the incredible strain relocation places on families.

"Dealing with the family" doesn't just apply to executive hires. It can be just as beneficial for hiring teenagers, for instance. Meet with the parents of any teenager you employ. Explain your business and the job their child will be doing. Tell them what you expect of the child as well as what you hope he will learn from the job. Let the parents know that you take your role as an employer quite seriously and that you will teach the child responsibility and excellent work habits. Emphasize that they should feel free to call you if they have any questions or concerns. Ponder this: What do you think these parents will do if the child ever considers calling in sick so he can go to the movies with friends?

CONDUCT A QUALITY ORIENTATION

Don't assume osmosis will handle assimilation. Although it is a cute cliché, you really can't teach someone how to swim by "tossin' 'em in the middle of the lake." Here are some ways you can make the process productive and effective.

Who Manages the Process?

Actually, you have a built-in advantage over your giant competitors. Because you are an entrepreneur, and I assume a much smaller enterprise than MegaGlobal, you will handle the onboarding personally. This avoids the biggest problem with most orientations: the employee's introduction to the company coldly administered by someone in the human resources department. Sure, it is helpful to involve some of his peers and different specialists, but go ahead and take full equity for this important process. Realize the huge letdown the new employee receives when, after being courted by his new boss (owner and entrepreneur), he spends his first day with a twenty-three-year-old intern. Here is a good process for you to follow for orientation.

Describe Your History

Begin with an overview of the job and the company. Explain its history, your vision, the services you provide, and a candid evaluation of your competitors. Tell him about the challenges you face, your great victories, and the many things you have learned from hitting some potholes along the way. In short, pull him into the culture of the company; make him feel as though he has been a part of your dream from day one.

Review Your Expectations

Have a detailed discussion of the job description for his new position. Discuss your performance expectations. Review goals he should have, both short- and long-term. Explain how his performance will be measured and evaluated. This discussion should clarify how he will know when he is doing a good job.

Explain Office Routines

Actually, you don't have to be too specific here; most of this will get covered as he meets with others. Take the time to review policies, rules, and any idiosyncrasies you have (unofficial rules that hold special importance to you).

Assign a Mentor

Every company has its own unofficial set of rules, nuances, and traditions. "Oh by the way" comments made during a marathon orientation sessions can easily go unheard. A stack of papers can easily get lost in the shuffle. I've pounded on the mentor theme several times, but I must underscore its importance. Do this and make the employee's life—as well as yours—easier.

Introduce the Co-Worker to the Team

If yours is a small company, arrange some time with each co-worker during his first week. Be positive and supportive as you make these introductions, and then leave them alone to exchange information about their roles and future interactions.

Have All Supplies Ready to Go

Make sure his office is fully stocked or has the tools needed to immediately get to work. There is little that is more frustrating than for an enthusiastic newly-hired plumber to be ready to jump right in and then discover he has no wrench.

It's Not Just a One-Day Thing

Here is what my analysis has shown from employee retention. If the employee stays for a year, you've usually got him for a lifetime career. And if the employee stays ninety days, you'll keep him for a year.

Why ninety days? It takes about that long to learn the job, the company, and the co-workers. After three months, the new guy is no longer the new guy and is an accepted part of the team. It is also about this time that the shine wears off for the employee. The honeymoon has long been over and life has settled into a routine. Our goal is to make it to that ninety-day mark.

Look for ways to enrich the orientation process, allowing the team member to become more fully ingrained in your culture and operations. One way to do this is to give cross-functional assignments or by placing her on a project that is completely outside her assigned job.

Occasionally send her on field trips. Touring a supplier's facilities, spending a day with the account manager at your advertising agency, or even riding along on a delivery truck will let the employee see your business from a different perspective. Another great assignment is to have her work with you in a booth at a job fair. These assignments, field trips, and exposures to unfamiliar areas will help ingrain your culture in her, as well as demonstrate your ongoing interest in her development.

FINALLY, CELEBRATE!

The long selection process has ended and the employment period has begun. Sounds like a couple of good reasons to celebrate. Make this a memorable occasion, not only for the new employee but also for your entire team. You can certainly plan a party during lunch or place a welcome banner above her new cubicle, but also look for other unique ways to celebrate the arrival of a new team member. Make this customized celebration part of your company's culture.

There is a story of a man who accidentally fell off the roof of a sixty-story building. As he passed a balcony about halfway down, a woman shouted to him, "How are you doing?" "So far, so good," the man replied.

You knew from the moment you dove into entrepreneurship that your success depends on the quality of the people you have gathered around you. If you follow the guidelines discussed in this first section, you stand an excellent chance of gathering a splendid group of talented people. So far, so good.

But just like that man spiraling through the air, the full implications have not yet been revealed. Those splendid employees are just payroll liabilities until they are molded into a well-functioning team. Let's take that next step and explore the art of teambuilding.

II

BUILDING YOUR TEAM

It's easy to build a team, right? All you have to do is collect the best people you possibly can and it will all work out. As an example, look at this group I assembled for a fantasy baseball game. You'll agree it consists of nine of the greatest players to have ever taken the field.

Warren Spahn	Greg Maddux	Roger Clemens
Bob Gibson	Don Drysdale	Tom Seaver
Sandy Koufax	Nolan Ryan	Cy Young

Yes, these are indeed great players, but those of you who know baseball also know that while I have certainly recruited incredible players, I have not built a good team. In fact, this is a lousy team that would never win a single game. Why is this? Other than the fact that half of them are dead, it's because all of these great players are *pitchers*. While some of them might be capable of fielding other positions, none of them could swing a bat or score any runs. It may be a good collection, but it is not a good team. There is more to having a great team than just having great employees.

Teambuilding is a tough subject to address because there are so many different definitions of the subject. This is further compounded by the plethora of approaches that can be taken to approach each definition.

We'll narrow our discussion of teambuilding by focusing on those parts most important to an entrepreneur. Accordingly, here is the definition of team that we'll work with:

1. A team consists of a diverse group of individuals having complementary skills and styles.
2. A team shares a common company culture.
3. A team works together productively.
4. A team focuses on worthwhile goals.
5. A team is based on a foundation of integrity.

My definition may seem incomplete and even contradictory. We'll address those potential holes by focusing one chapter on each of the five points of the definition. Let's begin by looking at my dysfunctional team of pitchers.

6

A Group of Diverse Individuals

You may find it oxymoronic for me to begin a discussion of teambuilding by emphasizing individualism. After all, the conventional approach to building a team has been to find people who are as *alike* as possible. In fact, employers frequently hire people based on what they consider the highest possible compliment: "He reminds me of myself when I was young."

The greatest teambuilding mistake entrepreneurs make is to hire team members who are like themselves. This was discussed in Part I; we saw how this hiring error could eliminate a lot of great talent and ideas. This error causes a lot of complications if executed within the walls of a large corporation, but the implications are much greater for the small business. The problem is exaggerated exponentially by an entrepreneur whose pride of ownership motivates her to shape her workforce to be a reflection of herself. Thus, she hires clones who certainly do reflect her strengths, but duplicate her weaknesses as well.

A department full of common weaknesses can be overcome by other departments, but if an entire *company* shares common weaknesses, then it should go ahead and have the company lawyer draw up the incorporation and bankruptcy papers simultaneously.

It's easy to see the need for diverse talents when looking at the baseball team I introduced in the section introduction. And I am sure no one will make the mistake of hiring a company full of nothing but chefs, programmers, receptionists, or lawyers (perish the thought). We won't waste time by discussing the need for employing a variety of skills or occupations. However, we will delve deeply into the more common—and devastating— mistake of hiring people who think alike and approach problems from the same perspective. Let's learn a system for identifying the various personality types so that you can develop a balanced team.

IT'S A QUESTION OF TYPE

Throughout your life, you have met people you immediately liked. Within seconds of meeting them, you felt as if you knew them, understood them, and they were the most competent individuals you had ever come across. Likewise, you have been with people who, no matter how hard you tried, you just couldn't make a connection. What is going on here?

These interactions happen when varying personality types meet. The people you immediately click with are probably your same type, while the ones you can't build a rapport with are from one of the other personality types. Let's do a crash course in personality profiling.

Since the time of Socrates, psychologists have told us there are four types of people. Ancient philosophers referred to these personality types as phlegmatic, sanguine, choleric, and melancholic. (You can tell no one consulted the marketing department before coming up with these names.) Other systems identify these same types but use terms such as fire, air, earth, and water; red, yellow, blue, and white; D-I-S-C; or NT, SP, NF, and SJ.

Though the systems use different terms, they all use the same concepts and tell us the same thing. I've combined the work of all these philosophers, psychiatrists, scholars, and hacks and created one rather easy system. I call this the CONTROL system, because it breaks the personalities into four groups determined by their yes/no response to two questions: Do they try to control others? Do they allow themselves to be controlled? The answers to these two questions break people into one of four groups. Let's call these four styles the Creator, Cogitator, Connector, and Commander.

To make it a bit easier to understand these types, we'll look at the men who served as presidents during the twentieth century, with special emphasis on four who served at the end of the century. Why use presidents? To make the point that no style has a monopoly on success. Each style has strengths and weaknesses, and each style can be used to have a successful career. Since many people consider the presidency as the ultimate symbol of success, I'll use it to illustrate the point. So, here to help with this little exercise are Bill Clinton, Jimmy Carter, George H. W. Bush, and Richard Nixon.

THE CREATOR

The Creator is direct in communication and open in expressing feelings. He is the person who comes up with lots of big ideas and enthusiastically sells those ideas. Creators don't just express an opinion; they also have a great story to illustrate their point. People are attracted to Creators: They appear genuine, approachable, and communicate brilliantly. However, Creators can be disappointing to some of the very same people they attract. This is because the Creator will bite off more than he can chew and rarely finishes any project himself. He is a visionary, for sure, but his participation often stops with the vision. A Creator appears to have many friends, but rarely are these friends very close. Most could be more accurately referred to as social acquaintances.

Creators will not attempt to control others and they are just as passionate about not being controlled. They will, in fact, shun the company of people they perceive as trying to run their lives, primarily because they have no interest in running the lives of others.

Notable Creators: baseball's Babe Ruth and Yogi Berra, Hawkeye Pierce in M*A*S*H*, Oprah Winfrey, Jay Leno, Regis Philbin, and Presidents Ronald Reagan, Teddy Roosevelt, John Kennedy, and Franklin Roosevelt (as well as George W. Bush).

Frequent occupational choice: entertainer, artist, firefighter, gambler, tour guide, activist, negotiator, advertising executive, salesperson.

Regional stereotype: California.

Leadership style: generates excitement and enthusiasm for the project, and judges people by how original they are in solving problems.

Strengths: creative, energetic, enthusiastic, and handles emergencies well.

Weaknesses: impulsive, puts too much on his plate, starts a multitude of projects but rarely finishes them, considers a project a done deal the minute he thinks of a brilliant way to solve the problem, likes to take credit and uses "I" a lot.

Focuses on: the idea.

Business quote: "Wait a minute; I've got a better idea. Why don't we ...."

When under pressure: gets sarcastic and defensive, and knows where each person's vulnerability is and goes straight for the jugular. If he feels he is being ignored, he will get loud and do other things that may call attention to himself. In extreme cases, he may even act in a bizarre manner.

Whimsical indications you are dealing with a Creator: drives a bright red sports car, dresses in the latest fashions, and supports the newest fads, and has a pet lizard, tiger, or some other exotic animal. His office is disorganized and features a lot of knickknacks, each of which has a "great story" behind them.

Bill Clinton Explains Creators

During the 1992 presidential campaign, the Clinton team had a slogan they used internally: *It's the economy, stupid!* His staff had to keep reminding the campaign to keep its focus, lest it stray into too many areas and water down its effectiveness.

Lack of focus is a danger of this type of management profile. While Creators are excellent at coming up with brilliant ideas, they also assume the details will take care of themselves. This slogan is also an example of how Creators can effectively deal with this weakness to meander. Clinton's staff was powerful enough to force the campaign to keep its focus even when the leader was prone to stray from the issues. He would have been well served had he kept this structure once he became president.

Because creators are focus-deficient, they may sometimes come up with ideas without preparing people for them. Bill Clinton provided us with an excellent example of this on his first day in office. While his campaign had zoomed in on the economy, his first official act as president was to declare that gays were to be admitted into the military. Where did that come from? Failure to focus is typical of Creators, because they fail to set the groundwork for their ideas.

Also, ideas may be impulsively announced and then abandoned because of the hassle that execution requires. (Universal health care is a good example of this.) While yesterday's idea is withering, the Creator is off announcing a new project.

Projects are often abandoned when their implementation generates opposition or requires strong logistical efforts to make them happen. You saw this behavior in how President Clinton approached his initial cabinet appointments. Many people were announced before their backgrounds were thoroughly checked. Some of them were quickly and unceremoniously dropped as soon as problems were uncovered or strong opposition developed to their appointments.

Another example of this trait can be found in one of the cornerstones of the 1992 campaign: Whatever happened to the middle-class tax cut? The answer is simple. The plan was too detailed to explain, too difficult to execute, and something much more exciting came along.

When left unchecked, "extreme" Creators can sometimes exhibit bizarre behavior. Because they so enjoy risk, Creators can ignore conventional boundaries and quickly cross the line if not properly supervised. The Clinton presidency gives us so many blatant examples of this that it would be a waste of ink to list them here.

A Creator can be a powerful leader, however, if aware of his limitations and if he takes steps to offset those limitations. Earlier, I gave an example of the 1992 campaign, when then-Governor Clinton had aides who constantly focused the campaign on one important issue—the economy. His aides (primarily George Stephanopoulos—a Cogitator, by the way) covered for Clinton's deficiencies while allowing his Creator assets—charisma and energy—to brightly shine through.

Another good example of covering for a deficiency also deals with the economy. Certainly, the highlight of the Clinton presidency was the country's unprecedented economic performance. However, critics ask, "What did Bill Clinton do that should allow him to get any credit for it?" I'll tell you what he did—he recognized that he wasn't capable of doing anything by himself, so he appointed Robert Rubin Secretary of the Treasury and reappointed Alan Greenspan as Chairman of the Federal Reserve. These two men (both Cogitators) knew how to handle the economy and Bill Clinton had the good sense to leave them alone and stay out of their way.

THE COGITATOR

The Cogitator is indirect in his communication and keeps thoughts private. Insofar as styles are concerned, she is the polar opposite of the Creator. Cogitators are very good with information and are outstanding planners. They are rational and humor-challenged. A Cogitator has a small but close circle of friends; these are usually people who are very much like her and with whom she can relate closely.

The Cogitator makes a competent leader as long as everyone voluntarily responds to her leadership. Cogitators tend to have the least amount of awareness of people having differing styles and think that their own style is so logical, why would anyone choose to be different? Because they are so introspective, Cogitators rarely try to control others but often find themselves being controlled by others.

> *Notable Cogitators*: baseball's Joe DiMaggio and Greg Maddux, Walter Cronkite, Star Trek's Mr. Spock, Star Wars' Yoda, The Godfather's Don Corleone, Mary Poppins, Sherlock Holmes, Bill Gates, most Jimmy Stewart characters, and Presidents Woodrow Wilson, Herbert Hoover, Calvin Coolidge, and William Howard Taft.
>
> *Frequent occupational choices*: bookkeeper, psychologist, scientist, novelist, mechanic, coroner, umpire, bureaucrat, and engineer.
>
> *Regional stereotype*: the Midwest (particularly Missouri, the "Show Me" state).
>
> *Leadership style*: develops detailed plans, thoroughly briefs subordinates on their specific roles, duties, and performance benchmarks, and judges people by how well they think things through.
>
> *Strengths*: thorough, balanced, fair, ensures projects are completed and done correctly. Organized, detailed, rational, and sensible.
>
> *Weaknesses*: gets caught up in the details and cannot see the forest for the trees, makes tail-wagging-the-dog decisions. Can spend so much time planning for contingencies that she never gets anything started, and doesn't realize some decisions just don't warrant detailed study.
>
> *Focuses on*: the process.
>
> *Business quote*: "Let me think about it."
>
> *When under pressure*: clams up, glares, and she seems to say, "If you don't care to hear my thoughts, then I will keep them to myself."
>
> *Whimsical indications you are dealing with a Cogitator*: smokes a pipe and has pet goldfish, his office is neat, orderly, and may have a family picture (with all family members dressed in their Sunday best). Charts and graphs may also be displayed.

Jimmy Carter Explains Cogitators

When asked what he could have done differently in 1980 that would have resulted in victory instead of being defeated by Reagan, Carter replied he would have needed just one more helicopter. How's that? Well, he sent five helicopters on the mission to rescue the hostages in Iran. Two were disabled, the plans only allowed for the loss of one, so the mission had to be canceled. If he had had one more helicopter, the rescue would have continued, the hostages would have been freed, there wouldn't have been all those "anniversary specials" about the hostages on television the day before the election, millions of people wouldn't have been angry about America being humiliated by Iran, they wouldn't have blamed Jimmy Carter, and they wouldn't have voted for Reagan the next day. Really. This is how Cogitators think!

And think they do. They look at every detail of every problem, probing every contingency. For instance, Carter bragged about having read every single line in the national budget. Their personal involvement in detail, combined with their exploration into all possible outcomes, can result in nothing getting started and long, drawn-out decision making.

Like other Cogitators, Jimmy Carter was famous for his icy stares. One aide commented that if he was angry with you, it appeared as though he was staring a hole right through you.

In 1980, Jimmy Carter wrote a book entitled *Why Not the Best?* The title refers to a placement interview he had with Admiral Rickover, in which Carter was asked, "Have you always done your best?" When he admitted he had not, the admiral coldly replied, "Why not?" This stuck with the young ensign and became the cornerstone of his management philosophy. Give 100 percent, cover all the bases, let nothing slip through the cracks. Detail, detail, detail. Explore every contingency. Perfectionism.

Harry Truman (a Commander) once lamented that the economic advice he received was usually framed as: "On one hand, this could happen; on the other hand, this could happen." Truman commented, "What I need is a one-armed economist." Cogitators would be better served if they had fewer hands.

How could Jimmy Carter have been more effective? We are seeing the answer right now. While Carter's presidency will be rated as below average, he is gaining a reputation as being a great ex-president. Interestingly, another Cogitator-president shares a similar fate. Herbert Hoover has been considered an ineffective president but a great ex-president. Both men excelled once they were able to pick their own projects, plan their priorities, and execute them.

Cogitators are not good at dealing with crises (note Carter with Iran and Hoover with the Great Depression), but left to their own agenda they can be potent leaders. Perhaps Jimmy Carter would have been more effective if he could have stuck to broad policy, allowed others to study the minutia, and relied on the advice of Commanders when confronted with emergencies.

THE CONNECTOR

The Connector is indirect in communication but quite open in telling people about her thoughts and feelings. You will learn a Connector's entire life story within minutes of meeting her. The most important thing to realize about Connectors is that they love to be surrounded by people and genuinely want to be friends with everyone. They carry a sense of tradition and have somewhat strict views on what is proper or improper, right or wrong. While Connectors are outwardly accepting, inwardly they can be somewhat intolerant and judgmental. Despite their outward good nature, Connectors will hold grudges, keep score, and find it hard to forgive.

Their indirectness causes them to make statements in the form of a question. For instance, if a Connector wants to eat lunch, he will say, "Are you hungry?" and if he wants to visit a retail store, he'll say, "Did you want to go to Wal-Mart?"

Connectors are controlling of others and are often controlled by others. Their controlling personality comes from a sincere desire for good things to happen for others and their overwhelming need to be caretakers. Since they genuinely feel they know what is best, they will attempt to influence others to act as the Connector feels is best for them. Because Connectors are compliant and willingly self-sacrificing, they are often easily controlled themselves.

Notable Connectors: baseball's Lou Gehrig and Dale Murphy, Mary Richards on *The Mary Tyler Moore Show*, Father Mulcahy on M*A*S*H*, Gandhi, Condoleezza Rice, and Presidents Warren G. Harding, Gerald Ford, and Dwight Eisenhower (as well as Abraham Lincoln).

Frequent occupational choices: minister, teacher, social worker, nurse, counselor.

Regional stereotype: The Old South.

Leadership style: gathers input from all team members, makes consensus decisions, and judges people by how hard they try.

Strengths: loyal, dependable, responsible, loves people and truly cares about them as individuals. Superb listener and an excellent person to bounce an idea off of, a team builder and a consensus maker, and extremely well-organized and excellent with details.

Weaknesses: more concerned with how things affect people than accomplishing the goal, can be overly sensitive, seeks so much input that she can be indecisive, quite resistant to change, sees things as black or white— gray does not exist, and may worry about, rather than solve, problems.

Focuses on: the relationship.

When under pressure: initially gets very quiet and may even sulk. The Connector will momentarily ignore injustices done to her but will not forget them. She collects them in a special place in her memory and will one day explode. God help whoever happens to be the one who adds the final straw to the camel's back.

Business quote: "Let's form a committee!"

Whimsical indications you are dealing with a Connector: serves as a Cub Scout Den Leader, even though she has no children, and has a pet puppy that curiously has remained a puppy for six years. Her office has lots of pictures of friends and family, and she'll want to explain each one to you. She chatters incessantly on the phone with friends while running errands, although feels so very guilty about using a cell phone while driving.

George H. W. Bush Explains Connectors

"Wait!" you exclaim. "George Bush was not the compassionate candidate. That was Bill *I-Feel-Your-Pain* Clinton. George Bush couldn't relate to anyone!" What we are studying here is the actual person, not the Hollywood creation or public persona. George Bush is indeed a man who pays close attention to the individual. He writes notes and letters constantly and, most importantly (to this trait), surrounds himself with many people to serve as advisors. Connectors have legions of friends, and no president has ever had a larger Rolodex than George Bush. (Here's great evidence of this: The closest thing Bush wrote to a presidential memoir was a collection of letters and handwritten notes that he sent to others, dating back to his college days.)

This style was quite evident during the Gulf War. Bush relied heavily on advice from many sources and was wise enough to ensure that these sources were of extremely high caliber. However, he did not stop at accepting advice; he also ensured that the war was backed by a consensus. Although it was debatable whether the Constitution required it, Bush first got congressional approval before acting in the Gulf. Then, he built a huge coalition of allies to support the war and had these countries contribute troops, equipment, money and perhaps, most important to a Connector, public support.

If a Connector's project is shot down or he doesn't get the contract, he will take the failure personally and feel he was personally rejected. You could see this response in Bush when he was beaten by Bill Clinton. Rather than face up to the political reality for his 1992 defeat, he was personally hurt by it. "I just don't understand," he would repeat in a sad, depressed—OK, *whining*—manner. He wasn't angry that Bill Clinton beat him: He was hurt the American people rejected him.

Connectors are valuable because they seek lots of input and build teams. The flip side of this is that they are often perceived as weak leaders because they rarely make decisions alone and never call attention to themselves. (Early in his presidency, George Bush had to deal with what was called "the wimp factor.") Failure to take credit for things and frequently using the word "we" is an admirable quality. However, it can be fatal for presidents.

THE COMMANDER

The Commander is direct in communication, even to the point of being blunt and insensitive. He keeps his personal feelings to himself, and it is difficult to read his mood. In fact, he is so good at this that he makes an outstanding poker player. He thinks of business as a contest to be won or lost.

The Commander craves and insists on power and is action-oriented. While this results in getting a lot of things done, it also means people are trampled over and their mangled bodies are left in the Commander's wake. A Commander has few friends but many business acquaintances with whom he has cultivated "mutually beneficial relationships."

The Commander is a controller, often to the point of being a manipulator. Unlike the Connector who controls someone in order to get the best thing for the other person, a Commander controls people for his own personal profit. Being in control is central to a Commander's psyche. Therefore, a Commander will never allow himself to be controlled and will react angrily to any attempt to do so.

Strengths: gets things done, doesn't accept excuses, has a strong goal orientation, grasps the big picture, can cut through the clutter and get to the heart of an issue.

Weaknesses: A Commander can be dogmatic and dictatorial. He likes to make decisions alone; in fact, he sees this as being decisive and a symbol of his competence. He rarely invites others to give him advice and believes asking for help is a weakness.

Focuses on: getting results.

Notable Commanders: baseball's Ty Cobb and Barry Bonds, General George Patton, Lou Grant on *The Mary Tyler Moore Show*, Andy Sipowicz on *NYPD Blue*, Vince Lombardi, J. Edgar Hoover, Hillary Clinton, Margaret Thatcher, George Steinbrenner, the Oakland Raiders (Just win, baby!), and Presidents Lyndon Johnson and Harry Truman.

Frequent occupational choices: military officers, corporate raiders, surgeons, police officers, and lawyers.

Regional stereotype: New York City.

Leadership style: makes decisions close to the vest, assigns specific duties and demands results, and judges people by what they accomplish.

When under pressure: gets angry, gets personal, gets even.

Business quote: "Just do it."

Whimsical indications you are dealing with a Commander: drives a Hummer, smokes a cigar, has a pet pit bull. His office has lots of mahogany furniture, a formal atmosphere, and his office door is usually kept closed. He doesn't greet you by asking, "How are you doing?" because he honestly doesn't care.

Richard Nixon Explains Commanders

No president more clearly defines a personality style than Richard Nixon does as a Commander. Looking at his presidency provides an almost exaggerated example of the strengths and weaknesses of Commanders.

Let's first look at how Nixon handled the decision-making process. Nixon was a private man, prone to sitting alone in his study, in front of a fireplace, putting pen to his ever-present yellow legal pads. He had the capacity for digesting and retaining enormous amounts of information, and his opinions were heavily colored by personal experiences he had throughout his long career.

Nixon had few advisors; he primarily relied on John Erlichman and H. R. Haldeman. Even their advice was limited, however. As smart and capable as they were, these two staff members spent an enormous amount of time serving as yes-men and in executing orders they had received from the President.

Nixon rarely had cabinet meetings, observing that it really did him no good to get the postmaster general's opinion on wildlife preservation in the Southwest. He preferred to make decisions himself and considered his knowledge base adequate for most of these decisions. Usually, he was right. Richard Nixon, like most Commanders, was unusually good at making decisions. However, whenever he failed to seek help that was needed, the results were disastrous, and stubbornness prevented Nixon from accepting competent help until it was too late. His eventual destruction was caused by this self-imposed isolation.

Nixon further exhibited Commander strengths and weaknesses in handling foreign policy. Nixon handled all foreign policy himself, removing most policy-making powers from his very capable secretary of state. Nixon handled all decisions from the basement of the White House; those decisions were executed by a very brilliant man, National Security Advisor Henry Kissinger. This relationship worked quite successfully until Kissinger began to attract attention to himself and became a media star. At that point, Nixon still worked with Kissinger (in fact, he promoted him to Secretary of State), but he was quite jealous of his new celebrity. Publicly, Nixon praised and honored Kissinger; privately, he mocked him and spied upon him. He kept Kissinger on a short leash and would not hesitate to cut his legs off when it was necessary to remind him who was the real boss.

Like other Commanders, Richard Nixon was hard to get to know and really had only one close friend. Ironically, even though Commanders have few friends and rarely show care toward others, they will defend their subordinates to the death, even when their subordinates are wrong. Commanders are more apt to refer to this as loyalty rather than friendship.

Under pressure, Nixon responded just like a typical Commander. A White House Enemies List was circulated early in his administration. This was a classic Commander move: Identify the enemy, watch him, and always be prepared to attack. Nixon even kept his own attack dog, Charles Colson, by his side to deal with those people and organizations perceived as enemies. This worked effectively for several years but was his eventual downfall. (I can make a pretty good argument that the entire Watergate scandal sprouted from this very relationship.)

How could the Nixon administration have been saved? What an incredible difference it would have been if Nixon had surrounded himself with advisors, especially people who were willing to argue with each other and with the president. Also, having a few Connectors around would have been nice. They could have cultivated some needed compassion, understanding, and teambuilding. Unfortunately, because Nixon surrounded himself with people just like him, he turned the presidency into a hardball contest and was eventually swallowed by the monster he created.

SO WHAT?

OK, that was fun, but what are we supposed to do with this information? Especially since the bottom line about the various descriptions is that all the styles seem to have flaming weaknesses!

This is actually not the case. I just emphasized (and exaggerated) weaknesses to make the point that there is no ideal style. Every style has been represented in the Oval Office by both successful and unsuccessful presidents. Every style is successfully represented in the boardrooms of major corporations, on the playing fields of great athletic teams, and behind the desks of every small business.

It's also important to note that no one is purely one style. The four groups listed represent predominant styles. Every person has exceptions to his primary style and exhibits traits more relatable to other personality groups. For example, there are Creators who are excellent with details and Commanders who are quite concerned about how others feel.

Also, no one is perfectly consistent; people will often react differently under changing circumstances. For instance, a Cogitator may very well have an irrational temper tantrum from time to time. Don't get hung up on finding the exceptions and variances. (Doing so will make this a tail-wags-the-dog exercise.) Learn how to group people by their primary style so you can quickly understand other's perspectives.

What can you do with this information? Let's answer this question by exploring four benefits of using this profile system: relationships, hiring, teambuilding, and leadership.

ENHANCE RELATIONSHIPS BY TREATING PEOPLE DIFFERENTLY

Understanding that people are different should result in approaching people differently. Let me provide an example based on gearing the style of your memo toward the recipient.

Let's say you are proposing a project to two department heads. One is a Commander and the other is a Cogitator. To the Commander, you should declare your bottom line in the very top line. State your agenda right from the start and then follow with the sentences supporting your request. If he agrees with your initial sentence, he'll approve your request. If he questioned it, he would keep reading the supporting logic until he had the facts he needed to agree with you.

The other department head may be a Cogitator, meaning she wants to see how you reached your decision. Remember, a Cogitator thinks the *process* is as critical as the *decision*, so write her a memo in the opposite way you wrote to the Commander. Begin by listing the problem, follow with several possible solutions, and conclude with the reasons you decided on your proposed course of action.

Note the tension you would create by reversing these styles. If the Commander received the second memo, he would think you were being tentative and wasting his time. However, the Cogitator might consider the "Commander memo" as being rash. She would fear you had failed to consider all reasonable options and merely jumped to a quick conclusion.

Understanding the nature of others is the key to successful communication. Learn to deal with people the way they need to be dealt with. This is not manipulation; it is showing courtesy and respect for the perspectives of others. Also, carry this forward to understanding the reactions of others:

- Be patient when a Connector wants to explain every detail of her plans when she is asking for a day off.
- Don't take it personally when your enthusiastic "Good morning! How are you today?" is met with a terse "I'm good," by a Cogitator.
- Don't be insulted if your Commander co-worker has no interest in sharing deep personal feelings with you.

Accept the fact that your Creator sales manager has to tell you a clever anecdote to underscore his point every time you ask for some quick data. It's just his nature.

HIRE QUALITY PEOPLE BY NOT EXCLUDING OTHER STYLES

You probably wouldn't consciously exclude someone based on his style, but subconsciously you would be drawn to selecting someone who has your same style. Studies show most employers make a hiring decision within seconds of meeting the applicant. Seconds! What is going on here? It is an example of the interaction of the personality styles. People of the same style tend to click immediately. They understand each other and can converse easily. If you are unaware of this fact, you could choose someone who matches your personality style, just because it "feels right." In doing so, you may hire an incompetent who fits your personality while ignoring many talented people who have differing styles.

Do you really want to hire people who are just like you? After a while, your whole team will be so inbred they will look like the fellow sitting on the porch playing the banjo in the movie *Deliverance*.

Here are some (tongue-in-cheek) consequences of having a team made up of a single style:

Connectors: Nothing will get done, but everyone will get along and know the names of each other's children.

Cogitators: Nothing will get done because they'll spend their time defining the process.

Creators: Nothing will get done, but you will hear a lot of really great stories.

Commanders: The job will get done once one of the Commanders has killed the rest and taken sole charge of the project.

BUILD TEAMS BY BUILDING MUTUAL RESPECT

Your team will not be effective if it consists of members who are all alike. Having diverse personality styles results in healthy, productive teams.

However, just hiring diverse styles will not create that positive alliance. In fact, turmoil is the most likely result if the styles are mixed without each member understanding their differences.

For instance, the potential for conflict is tremendous between Creators and Cogitators. The Creator considers the Cogitator to be too conservative, slow, and an obstructionist. The Cogitator sees the Creator as whimsical, flippant, and someone to be viewed with suspicion.

However, you can create a powerful team if each person is aware of, and genuinely respects, the talents of the other. The Creator will create great visions and inspire others to reach for that vision. The Cogitator will organize the project and ensure that all consequences are considered and risks are properly balanced. Most of all, the Cogitator will ensure that the Creator's vision becomes reality. The Creator will be relieved if she understands this about her Cogitator co-worker. The Creator will know she is free to think up brilliant solutions, knowing her partner won't let critical steps fall through the cracks.

In the opposite corresponding relationship, the Creator will motivate and energize the workforce, assuring that the Cogitator's well-planned projects are enthusiastically followed and the product is sold to the marketplace.

Another example would be the combination of the Commander and the Connector. Without understanding and respect, the Commander will run roughshod over the Connector and the Connector will resist any and all change. With mutual respect and cooperation, the Connector can ensure the Commander's goals are supported by a well-motivated team and that the team has been communicated with thoroughly. The Connector will also gather feedback and ideas, helping to make the Commander's projects better thought out.

LEAD POWERFUL TEAMS BY UNDERSTANDING TEAM MEMBERS' PROFILES

You can harness this power when you recognize that any combination of personality types can work together productively. In fact, you can build a powerful team if it is diverse and exploits each member's strengths and eagerly compensates for their weaknesses. The team will be far more powerful than if each member is a mirror image of you.

Imagine a team having one of each type in it: a Creator who comes up with ideas and inspires others to share the vision, a Cogitator who plans the procedures and evaluates risk, a Connector who builds the team and keeps them motivated, and a Commander to keep everyone on track and demands timely execution.

You could conquer the world.

7

Sharing a Common Culture

"Wait!" You are shouting. "First you emphasize the need for diversity and now you declare the team must conform to a single culture." Actually, these concepts are not contradictory. Diverse people can share basic beliefs and customs. Need proof? Just look at the faces in the crowd watching a Fourth of July parade.

Culture is a company's way of life. It is how the business functions, operates, handles stress, and reinforces its staff. It is the company's attitude toward the world and its image in that world. It is a big umbrella that can cover a lot of diverse talents, beliefs, and ways of thinking. In fact, not only can it handle individuality, it probably requires it.

As with so many things discussed in this book, you have an advantage over MegaGlobal in having a strong company culture. Because management is so far removed in time, rank, and distance from upper management, the culture in large corporations doesn't fully reflect its owners, founders, or even the current board chairman. However, because you are directly involved, see all day-to-day activities, and know your individual employees well, you actually have a better opportunity to influence a strong culture than your counterparts at MegaGlobal.

HOW IS A CULTURE CREATED?

The CEO of a large company attended a motivational seminar and was excited about a presentation he heard on the benefits of having a positive corporate culture. Returning to his office, he telephoned a vice president and told him of the experience. He then ordered, "I want a company culture, and I want to see it by Monday."

You may need more than a weekend, but establishing a company culture does not have to take decades. You can make major strides toward creating your culture *just by making the decision* about what you want the character and personality of your business to be. Let's look at the major influences on culture creation.

Company Founders

You are the strongest influence on your company's culture. As the founder and creator, your company's culture begins as a full reflection of you. You will establish your personality, methods, and values with the people you hire and the direction you give to them. Since you will probably be directly involved in the details of all initial decisions, you will establish the precedence on which all future decisions will be based. Your views will become the accepted norms in the organization and the basis for legends that will ripen in future generations.

Ray Kroc at McDonald's and Dave Thomas at Wendy's stand as examples of the strong influence an owner has on his company's culture long after the owner has left the scene. McDonald's still measures its performance based on Kroc's insistence of "good food at a good value, served in clean, family-oriented surroundings." Likewise, all future Wendy's managers will shape their daily operational procedures to deliver QSC—quality, service, and cleanliness.

Perhaps the biggest example of a founder's influence can be found at DisneyWorld. New rides, shows, even theme parks and hotels are designed around Disney's high standards and family focus. Decades after his death, Disney employees still settle arguments by asking, "What would Walt do?"

Your new company may never grow to the size of McDonald's, Wendy's, or Disney, but your influence on company culture can certainly be as dominant as Kroc, Thomas, and Disney were to theirs. Do not underestimate your clout in shaping the culture of your business.

Precedent

The next biggest influence shaping your company's culture is precedent. Your culture develops in response to the decisions it makes. This means that early decisions in the company's history carry tremendous weight in shaping its culture.

We can see the significance of this in our legal system. The U.S. justice system is based on English common law, which depends on looking at past decisions for making today's decisions. It has evolved from the Middle Ages when there weren't many laws governing the conduct of commoners. People were responsible for finding their own justice. You didn't call a cop if a neighbor stole your chicken; you simply went next door and took a stack of his firewood. This self-help was often difficult (such as responding to some unfairness from a more powerful or better-armed foe), and people began appealing to the king for justice. The king would evaluate each "lawsuit," and deliver his judgment.

This worked well. Perhaps, too well, because people began lining up early and the king found that he was spending all his time judging cases. In order to clear his calendar for more worthwhile pursuits (golf, serfing, planning invasions, etc.), he delegated dispute resolutions to some trusted subordinates. Since so many of these cases were similar and the king's decisions were consistent, the new judges learned to simply apply past precedents to all new cases. After the same decision was made a few dozen times, certain punishments became entrenched into the law. (Killing a chicken cost you two bales of hay, cruelty to a horse was twenty lashes, etc.) Thus, common events resulted in common punishments, and common law was established.

Granted, I have taken a long route to get here, but the decisions you make and the method you use to make them will establish a precedent. That precedent will influence—if not actually determine—every decision made in the years to come. For instance, if you instruct that all bills are paid within seven days, this principle will be ingrained as part of your culture. Years from now, a new accounts payable clerk may decide to hold checks for two weeks and he will be drowned in a chorus of, "That's not how we do things around here!" Future policies and procedures will not vary from the way things were done until something dynamic causes a change. (To extend the metaphor, it would require a Supreme Court reversal.)

Take great care in the decisions you make in the early years of your existence. It is so much easier to establish positive cultural values than to change them down the road. If you start out letting people run late for work routinely, you'll have a difficult time establishing a firm 8:00 A.M. start time. Ignoring rudeness to customers during the first few days your bookstore is open guarantees you will have miserable customer relations forever. As well, once a waiter sees that you tolerate poor-quality food being served, all of your waitstaff will inherit these low quality standards.

Fortunately the opposite is also true. Demand high standards initially and high standards will become a permanent part of your organization's culture. Whether good or bad, little decisions today will guide the major decisions of the future.

Internal Interaction

Similar to the way standards are established, the way your employees treat each other will always reflect the way they interacted initially. For instance, perhaps you hire your best friend as your salesman when you start your business. Since he is your best friend, you naturally spend a great deal of time with him, discuss problems, and seek his advice. Years later, after that friend has long been separated from your company, it would not be unusual to see the person occupying that sales position to also be your closest advisor. Other employees will perceive that job title to carry clout and significance beyond its written job description, despite whomever actually holds the position.

Likewise, how employees interact in the future is often similar to the way it was done in the early years. Whether the atmosphere is formal or folksy, discussions are respectful or hostile, or meetings are free-flowing or agenda-specific, all these cultural interactions evolve from a base established the first year of your existence.

TOOLS FOR ESTABLISHING CULTURE

As you can see, you can shape your company's culture by starting early and being directly involved. There are many tools you can use to direct its creation.

The Name

My wife and I took great care in selecting our daughter's name. We chose "Katherine," because it met all of our requirements: it was feminine and strong at the same time, had a rhythm in its pronunciation, and reminded us of positive qualities possessed by many past holders of the name. As we later discovered, our family lineage has a history of Katherines extending to the early 1700s when the Tanner's boat docked in Virginia (and an added bonus is that she also shares my initials).

While some of you may be thinking that I just have too much time on my hands, most of you are nodding with understanding. There is power and meaning in a name. Connotations often create destiny.

Look at what a name says about the company. Using your own name—as many consultants or professionals do—implies a pride in ownership and a sense of personal equity. Other names may suggest a sense of proper professionalism or indicate a degree of informality. (For instance, you would never want to use a name like "Bob's Law School.")

You can use your name as a cornerstone for your culture. Sonic Drive-In sends a message of definite commitment to fast service, not only to customers but also to its employees. What do you think the decision is whenever there is debate about adding a tasty new menu item that takes a long time to cook? What are the expectations from a repairman arriving in a truck marked Friendly Plumbing Services versus the law firm of Dewey, Cheatham, & Howe?

Symbols

Here is a bit of research you won't find surprising. People were asked for their impressions of different companies based on photographs of office decor. Those featuring lots of plants and flowers were thought to have friendly and cheerful workforces while those displaying trophies and awards were seen as employing high achievers. Carefully select your office décor to assure it reflects the image you seek.

This just scratches the surface. The building you choose carries equal impact. According to John Scully, former president, PepsiCo's world headquarters were designed to make visitors and employees feel they were seeing "the most important company in the world." To better symbolize security, banks are overbuilt to appear as though they could survive a direct nuclear hit.

There are more obvious symbols, of course. Perhaps the most visible is your choice of logo. Similar to your company's name, your logo visibly displays certain features of your culture. Recognize the impact made by your choice of colors and graphics.

Also, use slogans to frame your culture. Look at the expectations created by these:

- *Quality is Job One.* Ford Motor Company
- *When it absolutely, positively has to be there overnight.* FedEx
- *Progress is our most important product.* General Electric
- *An Army of One.* U.S. Army (My favorite, by the way.)

Yes, these are old established companies with old established cultures, but there is no reason you cannot create a culture-defining slogan right now.

Stories

Companies also transmit their cultures by retelling stories from their pasts. Events occur in the life of a company that serve as examples of expected conduct. Over time, these stories may gain legendary status, causing the message to forever determine decisions.

My favorite example comes from Stew Leonard's, a chain of food stores known for its exceptional customer service. They even have signs posted in all their stores saying *"Rule #1: The customer is always right. Rule #2: If the customer is wrong, re-read Rule #1."*

Employees still talk about the time Stew bought a tuna sandwich and found that it came with an extra packet of mayonnaise. Stew believed the sandwich had enough dressing as it was, so he told the deli manager to leave out the package in the future. On a visit a few days later, Stew once again found a packet of mayonnaise wrapped with his sandwich. His deli manager explained, "Sorry Stew, the customers want the mayo so I'm going to keep right on putting it into the package." Employees tell this story as an example of the company's insistence on pleasing their customers—no matter whose toes are stepped on.

So, you're thinking, "That's a great story, Ken. But we're not an old established company with a lot of stories archived in the folklore. In fact, we opened the doors yesterday and so far the only story involves getting a clog in one of the toilets." Granted, remarkable legends are scarce with new companies. So how can you make use of this great tool? *Borrow some stories from others.*

For instance, if you want to impart a concern for customer relations, tell them about a story that made a big impact on you that occurred in the deli of a grocery chain. Even though the events did not happen in your company, the principles they underscore will graphically explain the desires you have for your own company's culture.

Jargon

Established teams tend to evolve their own language. Government entities are liberal in their use of acronyms; the military quickly learns short words that communicate complicated, life preserving actions; and, according to the movie *The Godfather*, the mafia had some colorful ways to describe events, such as the classic saying, "I'll make him an offer he can't refuse."

It does take some time to develop an internal language. It probably won't catch on if you try to force the issue, but you can accelerate internal bonding by encouraging such development. For instance, police departments use codes to communicate over the radio. To protect an officer's safety they will say, "Code twenty-six," instead of announcing, "The person you are standing next to is wanted for assault." Many of these codes have crept into officers' everyday language. Even when officers are off duty, they will jokingly refer to a comrade by saying, "Signal 24" (insane person) or tell a friend he may have had too much to drink by saying, "You're about to be 28."

Using this type of terminology makes a person feel like he is on the "inside" and one of the guys. Look for opportunities to incorporate insider terms into your company's internal language. You can do this by incorporating insider terms into memos or dropping them into casual conversations.

Ceremonies

Identify and celebrate milestones even in the early formation of your business. You can mark the anniversary of incorporation or the rollout of a new product. Commemorate birthdays. Have a party every time you land a new client or receive a big contract.

However, you may consider kicking it up a notch by imitating Hollywood. The entertainment industry has taken worker recognition, added steroids, and developed a culture of self-congratulation that defies description. It would seem that every Saturday night from January to April is filled with a different method for recognizing and deifying people in the industry. Glamorous awards are followed by emotional, teary-eyed speeches exalting the recipient's incredible contribution to humankind.

I've wondered why only actors do this. In fact, if I were to rank occupations based on how they affect my quality of life, I'd have to place actors pretty close to the bottom (just above paper-clip designers). Wouldn't it be wonderful if some of the more significant workers—plumbers, receptionists, nurses, paralegals—were recognized with such gusto? I'd love to see a red carpet for teacher, firefighter, or administrative assistant of the year.

Duplicate Hollywood. Have an annual celebration acknowledging important events in your business. If your company is large enough, name a manager of the year and give awards to recognize customer service, the friendliest employee, cleanest store, or best suggestion-box submission. Hint: Choose categories that support your company's stated values and goals, not just sales performance.

Inside Jokes

I've seen every episode of the TV show *Fraser*. In fact, I'm such a big fan that I've actually memorized most of the plots and dialogue, and now amuse myself looking for little details. Here is a neat discovery: the opening title graphics are quite similar, but vary each season. While all episodes show a background of the Seattle skyline over the opening title graphics, there are some subtle changes made each year. One year will show a helicopter flying by; another will show a glimpse of the searchlight on the Space Needle. These are imperceptible to the casual viewer but with a sharp eye, one can identify which season a specific rerun was filmed.

You have to think that there was a reason for these subtle variances and it wasn't to draw more viewers. It was a little insider's joke, with the insiders being the production company and select viewers. This is a clever double-teambuilding tactic, recognizing their best "customers" as part of their team. (Also, look back at Chapter 3, *Focus: Setting the Right Tone*: I have a list of five people who don't know how to properly conduct an interview. Note the acronym formed by their initials.)

Look for an opportunity to have a feature about your business that is only for insiders to know. Share this "secret handshake" with your team and possibly some close clients. Let the bonding begin.

Attire

Dress codes are a way to boldly symbolize your company's culture. Just as an individual's choice of clothing says so much about him, the guidelines you set for workday attire says a great deal about how you want your company to operate. Your dress code should reflect the image you want to project to the customer. Accounting and financial firms can indicate their conservatism by dressing formally in dark colors. High-tech companies and sports agents may choose to suggest an informal image by dressing down.

Others have taken clothing selection to a whole new level through use of color. For instance, some police departments use a formal coat-and-tie uniform for court appearances, but short sleeve black shirts for field patrols. They may even take this one step further by dressing officers on neighborhood foot patrol in a uniform that is tinted in a color referred to as "approachable blue."

Not only does a dress style project an image to the customer, it can also shape your employees' job performances. I experimented with this many years ago in the fast-food industry. While most chains dressed their managers in colorful (almost clownlike) uniforms, I had all of my managers in a white shirt and necktie. There was an immediate change in their professionalism the moment they put on the necktie. Because they now looked professional, they acted professionally.

A local telephone call center uses a similar strategy. Even though none of their customers can see them, the company requires customer service agents to wear formal business attire. Just by hearing their voices, you can easily distinguish between this company's operators and the blue jean/tee shirt clad operators employed by others.

How do you balance the individual's needs for personal expression with a company's need for having a consistent image? Here is a system I like that accomplishes both objectives: Pick a style of uniforms and then allow the employee to choose a color or design. For instance, you may decide that your retail sales staff will all wear knit golf-style shirts and casual cotton pants, but each employee can pick from several colors of shirts matched with khaki or black pants.

While we are on the subject, I've never understood the concept of "casual Friday." You have established a dress code that serves to support your business image. If the dress code were crafted to project a certain image to clients, why would you want to project a different image on Friday? If we tell employees that casual Friday is a reward, then we are implying that the normal dress code is a punishment. If casual dress supports your image and motivates your employees, perhaps the exception should become the rule.

Show the Pride

Let me tell you about a recent family vacation. The Tanners packed up for the East Tennessee mountains and rented a nice cottage tucked into a hillside. There were many exciting and interesting activities that week, including whitewater rafting, roller coasters at Dollywood, and seeing a bear meandering through the Smoky Mountains. (We also took a boat ride on a five-acre underground lake. Our tour guide told us a remarkable fact: "This cave is 200,000,003 years old," he declared. "That's amazing," I responded. "How can they date its age so precisely?" He pondered my question briefly and then replied, "I really don't know, but when I started working here three years ago they told me it was 200,000,000 million years old.)

We had a great time on this vacation and did a lot of exciting things. Do you know what my ten-year-old daughter and her friend Emma enjoyed the most? It was a tour of the factory where Mayfield milk and ice cream are produced. I also enjoyed that visit, possibly for some other reasons than the girls had.

My enjoyment occurred at the visitor's center where logo souvenirs were sold and memorabilia was proudly displayed. There were photos of four generations of Mayfields and pictures of their home-delivery trucks from 1910. Advertising and news articles were proudly framed, and charts were posted that showed photos and breeding records of some of their prize cows. A model of a revolutionary contraption stood in the middle of the floor. (Invented in 1955, the machine removed all odors and odd tastes from milk, which gave the company a strong competitive advantage.) Outside the main entrance, lying under a shade tree, was a six hundred-pound bronze sculpture of Maggie, their award-winning "founding cow."

Another thing I enjoyed about the tour: the employees' faces. The tour guides showed obvious pride in their company, but I'm not talking about them. It was the faces of the line employees we passed as we walked through the machinery. They all beamed as they made eye contact, enjoying the celebrity. They were proud that they worked for a company that people thought was interesting and enjoyed the status that comes from being on display as an important part of that company.

Mayfield Dairy has done a remarkable job of displaying its heritage, creating a deep sense of pride in its employees, and in building even greater brand loyalty with its customers.

While you cannot match their creation today (after all, Mayfield has had almost a hundred years to build this heritage), you can certainly duplicate their intent. You can also celebrate your heritage, even if you have been in business for only few months. Here are some ideas:

- Display a model of the buildings or stores you will be operating.
- Hang your picture prominently in the lobby along with a group photo of your initial team.
- Place a mock-up of your product or invention in a display case.
- Keep a scrapbook in your lobby.
- Frame print ads and run them chronologically down the hallway. Also frame any news articles written about your new company; add to this collection as years go by.
- Are you a franchisee? Borrow the image of your parent company. Go ahead and hang a picture of Colonel Sanders.

Have fun brainstorming with your team and adding to this list. Spend the weekend gathering everything you can get your hands on and you'll have an impressive display of your heritage by Monday. Doing this will give you a strong ego boost, but also look at the impact on your employees. Overnight they will have gone from having a job with a new start-up company to being an important part of a firm that has a wonderful connection to its past. Then you can dream of someday having a six hundred-pound bronze cow lying outside your front door.

During my freshman year of college—1974—a couple of eager, tail-wagging entrepreneurs opened a new restaurant near the campus. Their pride of ownership was evident as a crane hoisted their sign above the modest building. Large bright letters announced the name of the new establishment, but I was amused by the words just beneath the business name: *Since 1974*. At the time, I just thought they were being tongue-in-cheek about the whole thing, but I had a different perception of the sign when I drove past it thirty years later. They were still in business and the cute joke had become a symbol of the company's remarkable heritage. My attitude shifted from amusement to deep respect.

There is more to building a culture. Culture also includes how your team works together, establishes its goals, and views its values and integrity. We'll include those facets in the upcoming chapters. But for now, just realize that building a culture is one of the most important (and fun!) parts of starting your own company. If you don't direct its creation, then it will sloppily evolve on its own. This is your company—a reflection of you. Be certain it represents you well.

8

Working Together

The reason you even have a team is so that you can reap the benefits of team members who work together. Indeed, you have wasted your time if you employ a brilliant group of individual performers who can't—or won't—work together.

There are many aspects to the process of having people work together. You could dedicate a lifetime of study to the subject and still not scratch the surface. Since we all want to dedicate our lives to other things, we'll just focus on the subjects most directly affecting you as an entrepreneur. As you begin to establish your team, you need to know and apply what is in this chapter: bedrock methods to encourage your employees to work together.

MOLD THE TEAM

Your employees will not work as a team until they feel they are a team. Show them how to behave as a team and equip them to function together. Here are the key points in changing their mindsets:

Show How They Benefit Personally

If you want to mold your employees into a team, you must first jump this hurdle: *People are inherently selfish.* You must show each employee that teamwork not only benefits your business but also her personally.

Fortunately, this is not difficult to do. Most people understand that a team is capable of producing more than the sum of its parts. (Sure, Lance Armstrong is a great bicycle racer, but he would have never won a single Tour de France without his amazing team.) Your company may employ a superstar salesperson, but he will never sell a thing without the support of the rest of your company's team. Build your foundation for teamwork by making sure all team members recognize their interdependence.

Treat Them as a Team

Abraham Lincoln once posed this question to a cabinet member: "How many legs does a dog have if you call his tail a leg?" The man replied that the answer was obviously five. "No," Abe explained, "the answer is four. Calling a tail a leg doesn't make it one."

Just declaring that your employees are a team doesn't make them one. You must back up that declaration by consistently treating them like a team. Here are some important ways to convey to your team that they are a team:

- Hold meetings to distribute news or information. Parceling out information to each individual team member destroys the whole concept of a team. It actually removes one of the great benefits of having a team—you lose the power of the great ideas and perspectives generated when people are together. Whenever practical, use this symbolic effort to convey that you consider your organization to be a team.
- State your goals and objectives from a team perspective. Show how all departments or disciplines must contribute in order to reach company objectives. Again, demonstrate that the power of a team means being greater than the sum of its parts.
- Then, find ways to compensate your team as a team. While individual salary levels must vary based on the position and the individual's qualifications, look for ways to tie bonuses and incentives to the team's performance on important projects.
- Motivate them as a team. Contests destroy the entire concept of a team. For example, a sales contest rewarding the top salesperson means that team members are competing against team members. For me to win, you must lose. You cannot build a team by asking people to work against each other. However, you can tap into people's natural urge to compete while actually building teamwork. Hold contests in which the team competes against a benchmark, such as delivering three new products to the market by year-end. Such a team contest still stirs their competitive spirit while it also encourages the concept of teamwork.
- Encourage members of your team to support each other. This seems obvious, doesn't it? Yet, look at this example of a system that had the exact opposite effect: The United States Navy once had a unique way to evaluate its officers returning from a tour. The captain of the ship was required to rank his officers' performance on that tour from best to worst. Someone had to be ranked first, even if all the officers had performed poorly. And someone had to rank last, even if every officer had been brilliant. The Navy abandoned this system in the late 1990s and for good reason: It discouraged teamwork in an "industry" that demanded it. Officers knew there were two ways to get a high evaluation—by performing well or by someone else performing poorly. Thus, the Navy had put in place a system that discouraged its military officers from helping out a peer. You can only assume that the only reason disaster was averted was because our naval officers had too much integrity to sabotage a fellow team member.

Many managers make a similar mistake. They will perform an exercise ranking employees from top-to-bottom on their performance. Even though the results of this exercise may not be revealed to the employees, it still poses a great danger for having a true team. While the team members may not be aware of this destructive process, the fact is that the manager is engaged in an anti-team activity. He cannot help but to think of his employees as a group of individuals rather than a cohesive team.

Before you can get your people to think of themselves as a team, *you* must first think that way. Forced ranking exercises will destroy your mindset and block efforts to build a true team.

Encourage Interaction

The purpose of having a team is to derive the benefit that comes from their interaction. Even though it is human nature to want to commingle, there are often barriers we need to knock down and activities to encourage.

Rearrange the Office

People will not work together if their office area consists of small cubicles with no common areas. Provide an office arrangement that, while allowing a place for privacy, encourages interaction and collaboration. Here is a great arrangement for this: small individual offices or cubicles that open into an inviting area, complete with a large conference table, surrounded by some comfortable groupings of chairs. Oh yes, don't forget the most powerful piece of equipment for encouraging interaction: the coffeepot.

Provide Effective Communication Systems

Communication may be quite simple if all of your team spends the day in an office arrangement like I just described. However, many businesses don't have such a nuclear arrangement. A salesperson might only be in the office rarely, or an operations chief may spend most of her time in your retail outlets. No doubt you have equipped these individuals with appropriate technology. Cell phones and the Internet do serve as tools for communication. I'm sure all of these individuals make use of these tools to communicate a lot, but who are they communicating with? Information loses much of its potential value when the only one receiving it is the individual's boss. Expect your team members to treat the team as "the boss." Stress the importance of keeping everyone informed. Have your outside employees get into the habit of copying the entire team on all pertinent (non-confidential) messages.

Encourage Camaraderie

People are more apt to collaborate as a team if they like each other. While a deep, personal relationship is certainly not necessary to do this, it does help if they at least enjoy each other's company.

Encourage activities that tend to help your employees bond personally. Sponsor social activities such as bowling and softball teams; organize a company picnic and outings to local concerts and events. Also, invite their families to participate whenever possible; this will create an even deeper relationship between your team members. Recognize the unifying effects of "breaking bread"—liberally use dinners and lunches as opportunities to build your team's relationships.

Practice Working Together

It takes practice for a group to learn how to work well together. Seek opportunities to practice those skills and build camaraderie at the same time. Involve your team in civic activities that will build their skills by helping others. Organize a food drive for the needy or participate in a walk-a-thon. Spend a weekend helping build a house with Habitat for Humanity. Check with the chamber of commerce for a listing of ways your business can have a positive impact on others while learning how to work together.

Hold a Lot of Meetings

Meetings have gotten a rotten image because so many of them are held as a routine, having no real purpose other than to fit into an expected routine. A gaggle of management consultants will tell you that the problem with most meetings is that they are poorly planned. I disagree. The problem with meetings isn't that they are poorly planned; it is that they are too *tightly* planned.

Get your team together often and let them get used to talking with each other. Use meetings as your primary tool of communication, replacing memos, e-mails, or any other medium not involving face-to-face exchanges. "Wait!" you are shouting, "Aren't meetings an inefficient way to distribute information?" Yes, they are, if that is all you are trying to do with the information. However, if all you want to use information for is to distribute it, then why even bother having a team?

Use meetings to improve the team's effectiveness and usefulness. If you have good news, bad news, or just plain news, call a meeting. They will all hear the information expressed in the same way, so the grapevine will be robbed of the confusion it depends on for its growth. Team members will hear answers to questions they were afraid to ask, and offer interesting perspectives, suggestions, and comments they would have otherwise not contributed. Yes, this is all so horribly inefficient but it is gloriously effective.

There are so many ways to use meetings positively, but let me share this one great way to use them for teambuilding: When Clint Clark was hired to turn around a lumbering fast-food giant, he scheduled biweekly meetings that lasted about ten hours. Over three hundred executives attended these meetings either in person or via conference call. Each department and operational area gave reports for the projects they were working on, the successes they had seen, and the problems they faced. Each report was followed by robust discussion, often including people who were not particularly experienced in the specific matter they were commenting on. (These, by the way, were often the most useful comments.)

On paper, these meetings would appear to be a costly excess. In reality, Clint used the meetings as an effective tool to bring the entire company together and have it operate smoothly. The people in new product development saw how they fit into the long-term marketing program. Operations in Florida saw the common issues in Colorado and Detroit. Everyone learned how they were contributing to raising the market value of the company as it prepared for an initial stock offering. In reality, the entire company learned to work together as one team.

Gather your team on a regular basis. Go around the room and have each person highlight their activities. Encourage them to offer suggestions, comments, and even condolences to their peers. Hearing about things—even when it doesn't directly affect them—makes them feel part of the team. Use this process to jump-start the adoption of a team mindset.

Another amazing thing will begin to occur during these meetings. You will start to discover *the gold mine in your cubicles*. During the discussion of one issue, a person from another department may share her experiences while working in that industry, about someone who may have once lived in a city in which you are considering opening a new office, or the employee in advertising may have had a previous career as a schoolteacher and can offer suggestions on how to train new machine operators. The fact is that your team members are so much more than the items listed in their job descriptions. Each one brings unique and valuable life experiences to the table. If you operate your business on a strict need-to-know basis, you will never tap into these wonderful resources. However, if you operate your company with an environment where everyone can be completely open with all their experiences (and are willing to listen to everyone's opinion), you will have effectively multiplied the capabilities of your team. Rather than being a costly excess, these open meetings are quite cost-effective, aren't they?

EMPOWER THEM AS A TEAM

Empowerment is a term that has near-cliché status in the business world. There is probably no single subject having more empty words written about it than empowerment. Most of what is written and taught is done in theory and for inspiration. Accordingly, even though deep in our hearts we know that we must empower our employees, we don't really know what it means.

Further, we fear that empowerment might not have boundaries. The loss of control is terrifying to most businesspersons, particularly the entrepreneur. How do we empower employees without losing control? These sensible questions and concerns often cause us to make a real mess of empowerment, often creating a situation that might have been better if left untouched. Let's use this section to clarify what empowerment really means and see how you can use it to make your team operate effectively.

Step One: You Gotta Believe

A lot of business owners merely pay lip service to empowerment, mainly because they don't really understand what it is. So, what is empowerment other than being a subject motivational speakers make a lot of money talking about? *Empowerment simply means giving your team the authority to do their work and put plans into effect to the extent you determine is appropriate for your business.* Empowerment does not mean you abdicate responsibility or grant renegade powers. A team is properly empowered when it has the internal capabilities to make decisions that you want them to make.

An empowered team will accomplish your goals and make your life easier. However, empowerment will fail if you aren't a true believer. It's tough to transfer power, especially for an entrepreneur who has invested her time, talents, cash, and soul into this dream. How can you let go of the decision-making process to a group of employees? The fact is you can't if this is how you perceive your employees. If you have followed the advice given in Section I of this book, chances are you don't think of them as just "a group of employees." You see them as quality professionals who are motivated to help make your business succeed. Never forget that these team members also have an investment in your success—their very own careers. Delay the whole subject of empowerment until you are a true believer in the concept.

Step Two: Establish Boundaries for Empowerment

This sounds like another oxymoron, doesn't it? It's not; boundaries are critical for both you and the team. You need to feel comfortable that your team is operating within the areas they can best contribute to your company. They also need boundaries to know when they can take decisive action and when decisions should be handed to you. Clear boundaries allow everyone to do their work more thoroughly, confidently, and comfortably.

So, how do you know where to draw the line? How do you determine what authority and responsibilities your team should have? I can best answer that by referring to my formula for authority: *You have authority over anything you are responsible for. You are responsible for anything you are given authority over.*

So, that leads to the definition of empowerment—giving your team the authority to handle actions you hold them responsible for. That's also how you maintain control over empowerment—by keeping that balance between authority and accountability.

Step Three: Explain Your Expectations

Whether you are setting up a temporary project team or just empowering your whole staff for ongoing operation, you must clearly explain what it is you want them to do. Explain the overview, how it fits into the big picture, and desired results. Encourage their questions, even if they are repetitive, overlapping, or bordering on the minutia. After you have explained it, have team members explain it back to you. Clarity on the front end ensures the group understands its direction, authority, and boundaries; they will be able to operate confidently without needing to constantly check in with you.

Here's a tip that has served me well: *Always explain why.* Explaining why prevents tail-wags-dog tangents. Better decisions are made if your team understands the purpose of the task.

Step Four: Equip Them for Success

Your team will not feel empowered if they constantly have to negotiate for the tools they need to do their jobs. In fact, the barrier that most often blocks a team's performance is wasted time acquiring the means to act. These tools include office space, access to management assistance, training, staff support, and money. (Very early in my career, I learned that the quickest way to kill a project was to ask for funding.) Give your team the tools it needs to accomplish the goals you have assigned.

Step Five: Let Them Make Mistakes

Your team members will flee from empowerment if they are micromanaged or if their mistakes are emphasized. Once you have delegated authority to a team member, do not second-guess her decisions. You should help her make better decisions by coaching and role-modeling, but—unless the consequences are devastating—do not change a decision an empowered team member makes. If you do undermine her, you will stifle her willingness to use her empowerment, as well as have the same effect on the rest of the team.

HANDLE CONFLICT

You have gathered a team composed of strong people. Strong people hold strong positions and will defend them, well, strongly. Thus, occasional conflict is inevitable in your team.

Not only is it inevitable, but it is healthy. Your team *should* examine all options, take positions, and defend those positions vigorously. They should also examine the positions others take and feel free to find holes in their logic. Failure to do so leads to shoddy planning and routine failures.

So, conflict is not, in itself, an issue. The real issue with conflict is that we are often so afraid of it that we want to avoid it completely. Rather than deal with it productively, conflict is swept under the rug. No rug is large enough to contain misunderstandings for very long, so differences, tension, and stubborn feet-in-concrete positions continue. Mishandling conflict can be the death of an otherwise brilliant team.

So, how can you corral this potentially healthy but often lethal tool? There are many approaches and techniques—you will spend your career perfecting your abilities to use them—but let me lay out three critical principles for caging this beast.

Confront Conflict

Many of us are averse to conflict and just hope that if we ignore it, it will go away on its own. However, like many diseases, conflict rarely disappears by itself. Ignore a conflict and it will get blown out of proportion, fester, and usually spawn a whole new line of designer conflicts that make the imagination tremble. When it comes to conflict, catch it early and deal with it completely.

Have Your Staff Memorize Chapter 6

How often have you seen people squabble about an issue only to realize that they all felt the same way? That's because most conflict does not come from a clash of ideas but from how those ideas are expressed. As we learned in Chapter 6, each of the four personality styles tends to approach a problem from a different direction and perspective. Teach them to appreciate and respect styles different from their own. Much conflict can be eliminated if each team member understands that what looks like disagreement is actually a concern over a different aspect of the project.

Search for Common Ground

There was potential for explosive conflict at one of my speaking engagements. I was the executive secretary for the local affiliate of Handgun Control, Inc. and had been invited to address a nearby National Rifle Association group. Although they were polite to me as I entered the room, I could tell they were "loaded for bear" and eager to chew me up during the question and answer session. I knew I was not going to recruit any members that night, but did see the opportunity to diminish the often hostile relations between our groups. So my introductory remarks focused on the fact that our two groups agreed on far more than we disagreed.

You are probably as shocked at that statement as they were. It is true; there is much common ground the two groups share. We both hate crime. One group believes there would be less crime with fewer guns, the other thinks there would be less crime if there were more guns. The difference was not in our goal; we both wanted to eliminate crime. The difference was in our approach. A few heads nodded.

Then, I pointed out that my group wanted to add twenty-five years to the prison term of anyone convicted of using a firearm in the commission of a crime. There was actually a scattering of applause.

I mentioned that I wanted to go beyond just understanding each other; I felt there was ground for cooperation. That statement raised its share of snickers until I explained that Handgun Control, Inc. did not propose the elimination of firearms. In fact, HCI actually believed that a citizen does have the right to bear arms. We just wanted anyone choosing to own a firearm to receive thorough safety training. Then, I suggested we work together to enroll gun owners in one of the NRA's excellent gun-safety courses. More heads were nodding.

I discussed several more areas of common ground that evening. While most of the question and answer session focused on areas of disagreement, even those items were peacefully handled with excellent dialogue from both sides. We actually had a constructive discussion instead of a shouting match—all because we discussed areas of agreement before dealing with the conflict.

If HCI and the NRA can have a civil discussion, anyone can, especially your team as it discusses whether to spend its ad budget on print or radio, the color of stationery, or the location of a new office. Be prepared to refocus your team whenever passions tend to run high. The team has probably lost sight of the objective; you will regain peace and make strides toward solving the real problems by reminding everyone of the actual issue to be discussed.

A team that learns how to handle conflict and channel it productively will be able to tap into the collective wisdom of the whole team. Be proactive on this issue and teach your team how to use conflict to improve the effectiveness of the team.

ENCOURAGE PEER LEADERSHIP

Here is how you will know you have built a solid team that knows how to work together: peer leaders will emerge. In fact, in order to work together most effectively, all of your team members must think of themselves as a peer leader. What exactly is peer leadership? Here is the best example I've ever heard.

In September 1982, the Atlanta Braves were flying home after the last game of the regular season. They were beginning a great celebration because they had just learned that their biggest challenger—the Los Angeles Dodgers—had just lost its game and the Braves were division champions. Adding to the excitement was that the Braves had won the division by the slimmest possible margin—one single game.

Dale Murphy was sitting in the middle of the celebration. Murph was the reigning MVP for the National League and one of the game's great players. There was no dispute that Dale Murphy was the best player on the Braves team. That is what made his next act so remarkable.

Murph sat for a moment with each of his teammates and made a short remark. "Hey Bob," he would say, "do you remember that catch you made in April that saved the game against the Pirates? That's the game we won the division by." Then, he would go to the next seat, "George, do you remember how you came into that game in April and struck out the side with the bases full of Mets? That's the game we won the division by." He would move to the next seat, "Dave, I'll never forget your ninth inning walk-off home run against Montreal. That's the game we won the division by.''

Dale Murphy had that conversation with every member of the team. It didn't matter whether the player was a star veteran or a bench-warming rookie. Murph could always remember one specific act that he had made to win one game, and that was always the one game the team had won the division by.

You can measure the progress of your team by noting this evolution of peer leadership. You'll know your team is beginning to work together when a peer leader emerges. You will also know you have a great team when *every* member becomes a peer leader.

9

Toward Worthwhile Goals

Several years ago, I drove aimlessly around the downtown of an unfamiliar city (which is another way of saying I was lost). I drove past the Wigs and Records Shop and then turned around in the parking lot of a general store with a sign announcing, *If We Don't Have It Then You Don't Need It*. The radio blared with a jingle from a KFC competitor who decided to make fun of the chicken giant's slogan by declaring, *At Bojangles, We Do Everything Right*. Finally, I located the business I was seeking, Bob's Laundry, Acupuncture, & Law School (OK, I made up that last one). I was left with the odd feeling that the world was terribly unfocused.

This episode reminds me of my favorite thing Yogi Berra never said, "If you don't know where you are going, how will you know when you get there?" You just can't dispute that kind of logic, but many business leaders do.

Entrepreneurs are especially vulnerable to such aimless wandering. That's because the early years are lean and scary, often so scary that just keeping the doors open for one more month is considered a victory. So the temptation can become overwhelming to stray from original ideals and pursue anything that can make or save a buck.

You understand this folly: An unfocused business expends all its intellectual capital toying with tangents rather than exploiting the niche that prompted the enterprise in the first place. You started a business for a reason. While you began your dream with a clear goal in mind, circumstances may have caused that goal to become hazy. Know that if your vision has become blurry, your employees are even more confused. You are asking them to hit several targets but giving them but one arrow.

Let's discuss the subject of focus. Good management practices require that you give your team clear direction. They must know what their target is. So how do we focus your team? We'll begin with a brief review of a tool you know well—the mission statement.

THE MISSION STATEMENT

Nothing focuses your business on a worthwhile goal better than the mission statement. When thoughtfully prepared, the mission statement will capture the essence of your business's goals as well as the passion that preceded the creation of those goals.

The mission statement takes the concept much further by explaining what your business is all about to your customers, suppliers, your community and—most importantly—your team members. A good mission statement is to your business what the Preamble to the U.S. Constitution is to our country—a bold statement of principle and character from which all the operating procedures and goals are birthed. A mission statement will help you and your team focus on a common goal and give everyone a benchmark to gauge performance.

After reading that statement, you are no doubt shouting, *Man I gotta get me one of them!* So you ask, "How do I produce a good mission statement?" The answer is: I'm not going to tell you.

Let me explain. Volumes have been written on this subject. Excellent guides are readily available, and good instruction can be found for free on the Internet. I will point you to these sources for all the technical instruction you could ever want for writing a mission statement and reserve this space for simply adding some good tips on managing the process.

Involve Your Whole Team

The process of writing the mission statement can be as healthy and energizing as the actual finished product. Having your employees develop the mission statement is a remarkably effective teambuilding exercise because they will learn to contribute, discuss, and even debate important principles that they will live by. When I say *involve your employees*, I do mean *all* your employees—no committees, no executive conferences, not just those who volunteer—every single person who draws a paycheck must be fully involved in the process. This will not only teach them how to work together and provide a terrific orientation, but it will also establish the personal equity you need to have a true team.

Involve Others Connected to Your Business

Invite friends of your business to take part in the process—key suppliers, your banker, your insurance broker, and even your ex-boss could contribute to the process. There is great value in hearing observations from people viewing you from the outside.

Peek but Don't Copy

It's great to use other company's mission statements as examples and to get ideas, but don't copy theirs. There is no value in trying to use other people's goals in order to reach yours. (Business goals and principles are like snowflakes and fingerprints in this regard.) Copying other company's mission statement makes as much sense as using another person's résumé.

Defy Conventional Wisdom

How many times have you seen *that* advice in this book? Here it is and for a darn good reason. Ignore advice telling you that there is a specific format, number of words, or specific subjects that must be covered. Yes, some mission statements can be expressed in a brief sentence, but yours probably cannot. Forcing a mission statement into a predetermined format or length turns the development of a mission statement into a tail-wags-dog ritual. You want to create a living, breathing document that will guide your business, not win a haiku contest. Remember: There is no Pulitzer Prize for mission statements.

Produce It over Time

A good mission statement cannot be rattled off in one sitting. Remember that the *process* is often as beneficial as the product itself. Work on it in one- and two-hour bursts for a couple of times per week over several weeks. Consider having a staff retreat or off-campus meeting to pull it all together after several weeks' deliberations.

Stretch but Don't Fantasize

Good goals will stretch your talents and should certainly be ambitious. However, if you want your mission statement to be taken seriously, it must be realistic and attainable. It's OK to declare that you will pursue aggressive growth, but don't say that you intend to be the country's largest real estate company in one year. People will work hard for ambitious goals, but won't even play the game if they are unattainable.

Post It, Live It

Once you have crafted your mission statement, you should shout it from the mountaintops. Post it in all work areas, include it in brochures and, if it will fit, print it on the back of everyone's business card. Give rewards to any employee who can recite it from memory. Quote from it to support your business proposals. Have a copy professionally printed, framed, and displayed in your entrance lobby where clients and employees see it every day. Your team members will be reminded of what your goals are and the critical role they play in achieving those goals.

Periodically Call a Constitutional Convention

Once every year or so, pull the team together and examine your mission statement. Do changes need to be made? Don't be afraid of this; sometimes, businesses need to shift focus. The mission statement should support your business, not control it. Change it if parts no longer support those goals.

No changes needed? Then just enjoy the benefits you derive by gathering all your people for a wonderful discussion of your mission statement. This annual review will be especially beneficial to new employees who didn't get to participate in its development.

MAKE THE MISSION STATEMENT COME ALIVE THROUGH GOAL-SETTING

You can derive even more power from your mission statement by letting your team members mold it to set goals fitting their particular talents and passions. Let me tell you about a method I used in a past life when I encouraged restaurant managers to create their own goals while staying within the organization's mission.

A key ingredient of the company's mission statement was "to provide an excellent experience for every customer." How did we measure this performance standard? We looked at four areas, represented by the initials Q-S-C-H:

Quality: Is the food made according to the recipe and served correctly?

Service: Is the order served quickly?

Cleanliness: Is the restaurant clean and sanitary?

Hospitality: Are the employees courteous?

Then, each of these areas was scored with a grade like in school: A, B, C, and F.

A: Far exceeds expectations; difficult to find any areas to criticize.

B: Quite good; a customer would be impressed.

C: Meets expectations and all standards; no areas of complaint.

F: Unacceptable; does not meet minimum standards.

These grades would be combined to describe a restaurant experience. For instance, an AFAF would describe great food and sparkling facilities, but some crabby employees took a long time delivering the order. On the other hand, a BBBB evaluation indicated an excellent experience.

Whenever I was invited to a district meeting, I would give the managers this challenge: "I'll give you one A, two Bs, and a C. Decide on what your priorities are and the character of your restaurant by arranging these scores to describe how you want your restaurant to operate."

Managers would immediately declare their goal was to receive an AAAA grade. "Not possible in theory or reality," I would explain. "To achieve an A you have to make the area a top priority, and it's not possible to make everything a top priority." After a few more squabbles over terms, the managers would eventually accept the parameters I had set up. There was great discussion and even debate as each manager presented his or her choices and reasons for making those choices. (I learned something about each manager by observing where she chose to place the *A*. Quality? The manager was a stickler for detail. Service? An excellent organizer and trainer. Cleanliness? Pride of ownership. Hospitality? Great HR skills.)

What did this exercise accomplish? I stated that even though the company's goal was to "provide an excellent experience for every customer," the managers had the freedom to take whatever path they chose. "While you must meet all standards in every area, you are welcome to prioritize any areas you wish." I went on to explain that while they could pick their priorities, they would only meet their goals if they told their team the path they had selected. We concluded the day by having each manager outline his strategies for achieving the rating he had declared. Each manager promised to meet with his team, explain his goal, and motivate his employees to support his goal.

Find a way to create a similar exercise for your business. Perhaps my program doesn't fit nicely into how your business operates, but it can be adapted. For instance, list points in your mission statement and ask each team member to pick one part that means the most to him. While continuing to support all parts of the mission statement, the area chosen will become their *personal* focus. It will become the facet they emphasize and could very well become an area in which they become the "company expert."

A WORTHWHILE GOAL

Everyone wants to be a part of something big. As an entrepreneur, you will realize that you don't have to cure cancer, fight crime, or establish world peace to have a worthwhile goal. Building an honest business, selling a helpful product or service, and helping your employees in their career growth are noble undertakings worthy of respect and admiration.

Your team members can also feel this same satisfaction when you involve them in the design of your goals. Let them see your dreams and volunteer how they can contribute their talents to help reach your business's goals. That process—that feeling of contribution—will make them feel a part of something noble and good.

Explain your dreams. Invite your team to wrap their arms around the real spirit of your business. Involve them in developing your goals, strategies, and tactics. You will find that your goals become their goals; that, in itself, makes them a part of something big.

10

A Foundation of Integrity

We all have our own definition of ethics. Some people consider ethics simply to be what is legal, while an equal number define it as good versus evil. A code to live by, standards of conduct, a reputation for integrity, the golden rule—all are terms we use to talk about the subject. Ethics is often viewed as a philosophy, an intangible, a subject for interesting conversation, but not as a tangible subject that is part of business-building like finance, sales, or accounting.

Indeed, that was the prevailing attitude toward ethics until recently. The *Exxon Valdez*, confusion over the definition of the word *is*, Enron, Arthur Anderson, Martha Stewart, WorldCom—and the list goes on ad nauseam—have taught us that ethics and integrity are not issues for Sunday School. They are tangible issues for the boardroom.

This subject is also a crucial part of developing your team. Many companies have crumbled making poor decisions that can be traced to unethical roots. There are also companies that have been saved from certain death just because founders instilled a concrete ethical foundation.

The early stages of building your business are the scariest, most exciting, and busiest moments of the entrepreneurial experience. It seems like there are too few hours in a day. It is understandable if you choose to fill those hours with the tangible decisions, such as finding clients and suppliers. However, your chance to set that ethical foundation that may very well decide the success of your organization exists in the early stages of your business development. As you build your team (who are, in reality, also founders of your company), find the time to tell them your ethical standards. It may be the most worthwhile planning you do. Use this chapter as an outline for those discussions and defining the character of your team.

REAL ETHICAL DILEMMAS

While every business school offers courses in ethics, I'm just not sure if the subject can be taught from a textbook of case studies. You have seen those quizzes that present scenarios and challenge you to select the most ethical response. I've scored 100 percent on all these quizzes; so has everyone who has taken them—my daughter's hamster would, too.

It is fairly easy to make the right decision for others. Right and wrong are easy to distinguish when you have no personal equity in the situation. That is why it is so easy to choose the right answers in the case studies presented at seminars. The issue with ethics is not knowing what is right or wrong. Ethical decisions involve a willingness to suffer consequences for making the right decision. Ethics are most tested when it is your neck—not someone else's—that is on the line.

When I say *your neck is the one on the line*, I need to add that your neck must truly be on the line. The personal consequences of doing right must be more severe than the benefits of doing wrong. Here's what I mean: You are out of the office with your boss when you stop at a convenience store. You pick up a pack of gum, or whatever, and hand it to the clerk along with a five dollar bill. The clerk mistakenly gives you change for a ten dollar bill. There is no question that the ethical thing to do is to point out the error and return the extra money. Undoubtedly, you would do just that. You would never even contemplate keeping the change or tolerate the argument that you could in good conscience keep the change since the merchant was the one who made the error and they could write off the shortage to "just a cost of doing business."

This is not an ethical dilemma because you actually receive a greater benefit by doing the right thing than by keeping the money. How's that? First, there is no real benefit to keeping the money. The extra money won't change your life. However, look at the benefits of returning the extra money. Your boss will think so much more of you when he witnesses your display of honesty. The clerk will thank you profusely and loudly declare how honest you are. People standing nearby will express their approval and you will feel good about yourself. If Hollywood were producing this scene, you would have a chorus of angels heralding your name in the background. Nope, there is no ethical dilemma here. There is no risk; there are no consequences.

Consider the same situation if you are offered a thousand dollars to throw a contract to an unqualified vendor. Is this an ethical dilemma? No. You will get far more of a career benefit for reporting the vendor than you would from the economic benefit of pocketing the grand. No courage needed here.

That is not where the trouble brews, is it? Challenges arise when we are most vulnerable—shouting their benefits while casting risk inside a hazy shadow. There are some very real barriers blocking the road to ethical decision making. Let's look at some of these barriers.

Hypocrisy

A Tennessee state representative was a master of explaining away apparent hypocrisy. He fought for price controls on milk but opposed them on liquor. "I've got 423 dairy farmers in my district," he confided, "and I've got to rise above principle."

Walking the talk is the greatest life challenge for some folks. It is very easy to say the right things, but it's a bit tougher to do them. Hypocrisy is the second biggest destroyer of leaders. (Pride, the number one killer, will be saved for another day.) Hypocrisy removes your platform, destroys credibility, and takes away your future leadership rights.

Tolerance

Tolerance, taken in its intended form, is indeed a virtue. It means to accept others who approach life in a different way. As I understand it, there's more than one way to skin a cat. We should tolerate alternate forms of cat-skinning that may vary from our preferred method. However, the concept of tolerance has expanded beyond cat-skinning. It now encompasses every activity for using a cat that one could possibly comprehend.

I firmly believe that if you can't whistle it, it's not a song, but I must be tolerant of the strange sounds being emitted from other people's radios. We should tolerate people putting ketchup on mashed potatoes. You should be tolerant of your daughter's new boyfriend with the orange hair. We must even accept the fact that some people do not vote correctly. That's tolerance.

In its current usage, tolerance is not an ethical virtue. Today, tolerance means having no standards whatsoever. Everything is to be considered acceptable and to feel otherwise makes you—gasp!—judgmental. Americans are so afraid of being labeled as intolerant or judgmental that we have warped into a society with few boundaries.

William Bennett addressed misuse of the word *judgmental* when he said: "Without being judgmental, America would never have put an end to slavery, outlawed child labor, emancipated women, or ushered in the civil rights movement. Nor would we have prevailed against Nazism and Soviet communism, or known how to explain our opposition."

Do not cast aside your ethical core just because the PC police say you are being intolerant or judgmental. This kind of criticism is just a subversive way to undermine your core ethical standards.

The End Justifies the Means

Here are some questions to ponder over your second cup of coffee:

- Should the CIA be allowed to torture terrorists to find out information that may save the lives of American soldiers?
- Would you accept an illegal campaign contribution if doing so would guarantee the election of a leader who would accomplish great things?
- Would you fire an innocent worker if, by doing so, you would save the company's very existence?
- Would you drop a nuclear bomb on Hiroshima, killing 150,000 men, women, and children, to save the lives of a million soldiers?

- Would you cover up an isolated mistake that would destroy the career of a medical researcher who is otherwise destined for incredible life-saving future discoveries?

I would not hesitate to perform some of these acts. I would never consider others, and for many, I just don't know. Frustrating, isn't it?

Justification

> Sure, it's going to kill a lot of people, but they may be dying of something else anyway.
>
> —Othal Brand, member of a Texas pesticide
> review board, on chlordane

Tough ethical issues are not new. *Time* magazine did an exposé forty-five years ago on the growing issue of conflicts of interest. An ethical lapse was causing stockholders to lose confidence in their companies and bosses to question their employees' morals. One Chicago businessman went so far as to have private detectives conduct periodic checks on his two hundred executives. He explained that if someone appeared to be living above his means, he would have him checked out. However, the businessman was having some complications enforcing this newly discovered concern for ethics. He explained, "I've got a couple of department heads I'm suspicious of now, but their departmental results are so good I keep my mouth shut."

We are often strict about integrity until it begins to interfere with our interests. Many people will jettison firm ethical standards as soon as they feel a bit of pain. For instance, people who feel underpaid will often justify embezzlement. In good conscience, they can convince themselves they are only taking what they fairly deserve. This happens in retail stores, restaurants, and expense accounts all across the nation.

You would never do such a thing? Have you ever embellished an expense report? No? How about fudged a bit on taxes? I probably hit a little closer to home on that one.

FAILED TOOLS FOR ETHICAL DECISION MAKING

Now that we've looked at some of the more popular roadblocks to integrity, let's look at some of the tools we turn to for help in making ethical choices. Here are some of the more popular roadmaps. Unfortunately, they can sometimes cause more confusion than resolution.

Right and Wrong

We are raised to know right from wrong. That makes it easy to make decisions in a black and white world, but this world features a lot of gray. Absolutes are hard to find, even for things we know to be true. Consider these absolute truths:

Cheating Is Wrong

The Sting won the Best Picture Academy Award in 1973. Audiences cheered as characters played by Redford and Newman robbed a gangster who had earlier killed a good friend. The movie's message: It's OK to cheat a cheater.

Stealing Is Wrong

No one faulted people stranded by Hurricane Katrina when they looted grocery stores for food, water, and baby formula.

Lying Is Wrong

Follow the adventures of contestants on the TV show *Survivor*. The rules of the game allow lying. So, is it unethical to lie when the rules allow it?

Let's consider the sad case of Susan Smith: In 1995, Susan Smith claimed her children had been kidnapped by a young black thug during a carjacking. The entire community helped search for the children and the evil man who had committed this crime. Sheriff Howard Wells of Union County, South Carolina, suspected Smith's story was a fabrication. Racial tensions were beginning to boil in this normally harmonious town, and he needed to extract a confession so his county could begin to heal. Sheriff Wells met with Susan at their church. As they sat facing one another, Wells told her that he knew her story was a lie. He explained that he had been investigating a drug ring and had posted undercover detectives at the intersection at the time Susan said the carjacking occurred. They had seen nothing. Susan asked the sheriff to pray with her, and then confessed. "I am so ashamed, I am so ashamed," she repeated as she exonerated the fictitious carjacker, detailed her actions, and showed him where the children's bodies could be found. Harmony and peace eventually returned to Union County because Sheriff Wells had been able to determine the truth. The irony is that the truth was uncovered with a lie. There was no drug investigation. There were no detectives. It was all a lie based on the sheriff's hunch. The sheriff lied and no one will fault him for it. It was the right thing to do.

Is It Legal?

Oh what folly we soon face when we look to the laws of man for ethical guidance. It is a sad fact that obeying the law does not necessarily ensure integrity.

Here is an example: Bribery is not only legal in some countries, it is customary. While it is legal to bribe those government officials, you cannot consider yourself to have integrity.

Also consider some situations in our own back yards: It is legal in many states to secretly record telephone conversations. Most municipalities allow retailers to hold gimmicky "Going Out of Business" sales without actually going out of business. Right-to-Employ laws in the South and Midwest permit you to fire a thirty-year employee without warning or any cause whatsoever. Heck, up until the 1950s, Louisiana laws allowed husbands to shoot a cheating wife if he caught her in bed with another man. (However, please note that wives were not permitted to shoot their husbands when found under similar circumstances—a double standard whammy.)

Our laws permit many unethical acts, but that does not make them ethical. Here is an important truth: *Just because you have the right to do something doesn't mean it's the right thing to do.*

Codes of Ethics

Many businesses and professions have developed a code of ethics. Sometimes these are included in a broad mission statement; often they are memorialized as stand-alone documents. Here is my favorite: "We are dedicated to conducting business according to all applicable local and international laws and regulations, including but not limited to, the US Foreign Corrupt Practices Act, and with the highest professional and ethical standards." That gem comes to us from the Enron Corporation.

The obvious point is that ethics requires more than lip service; ethics must be lived. Does this have any practical application? Isn't this really just a feel-good exercise so that executives can look noble? Let's look at a company that takes its ethical commitments as sacred—doing so probably saved its very existence.

Before its crisis, Tylenol was the absolute leader in the painkiller field. It had over 100 million users and was responsible for about 20 percent of parent company Johnson & Johnson's corporate profits. We are talking about a big business.

During the fall of 1982, a still-unknown person unscrewed the top off several bottles of Tylenol Extra-Strength capsules and replaced them with cyanide-laced capsules. The bottles were then placed on the shelves of six drug stores in the Chicago area. Seven people, including a child, suffered horrible and unnecessary deaths.

Within an hour of the discovery, Tylenol's president made a hundred-million-dollar decision and immediately ordered every capsule off the shelves across the nation. He then requested customers return any product they had for a full refund. This amazing reaction was well received by the public, which had been conditioned to expect corporations to deny liability and retreat behind an ivory wall of silence. Johnson & Johnson not only survived this crisis, but their actions help further cement the company's sterling reputation.

When asked how he could have made such an enormous decision so quickly, Tylenol President Don Meyer commented, "It is always easy to do right when you know ahead of time what you stand for." As it so happened, Johnson & Johnson had created a mission statement several years earlier that included a commitment that the company would "operate with honesty and integrity." When the crisis occurred, Meyer had no problem in deciding how it should be handled.

So, what good is a code of ethics? Is it a superfluous boilerplate like it was at Enron? Or is it near-sacred moral code as with Johnson & Johnson? The answer is that a code of ethics is as useful or as useless as the company and its employees want it to be. Having one ensures nothing. Making your code a part of your standard operations procedures is the only way to make it more than ink on parchment.

MAINTAINING INTEGRITY

Ethics can erode over time. For instance, deception begins as an innocent white lie, grows through convenience, further expands as we justify protecting others, and eventually becomes a standard part of our character. While I have indeed encountered a couple of characters who actually found a way to cheat at the game rock-paper-scissors, few people are truly evil. What happens is that their values erode over time. You don't notice the incremental slide. It's like obesity. At what point do you realize you're fat?

Thomas Carlyle wrote: "Make yourself an honest man and then you may be sure there is one less rascal in the world." The fact is ethics and integrity must be maintained as painstakingly as they are developed. Here are some ways to do that:

Tell the Truth

When my daughter Katherine was about four, I noticed her stories were growing beyond tall tales and creeping into the category of lies. Wanting to nip that character flaw in the bud, I read her the story of the boy who cried wolf. She enjoyed the story and had me read it several times. I figured I had made my point and wanted to verify that I had done so. "Do you know what that story tells us?" I asked. "Yes, I think so," she replied. "You can only tell the same lie twice."

Mark Twain explained a practical reason for telling the truth: You just don't have to remember so much. That is a good point because good liars must have great memories. Not only do you need to remember all the subtle details that make up a good lie, but you must remember which variation you told to each person.

HONOR YOUR COMMITMENTS

> The president has kept all of the promises he intended to keep.
> —Clinton aide George Stephanopoulos speaking
> on *Larry King Live*

According to a Jewish proverb, you must let your ears hear what your mouth says. The best way to ensure that you do what you say is to keep track of your commitments. Use your day planner to record what you have promised others. Whether that commitment is "I'll get back to you," "I'll be there," or even the old sidestep, "I'll think about it," record a definite time that you will deliver the commitment. Having an unfailing follow-through on commitments builds your reputation for trust.

ALIGN YOURSELF WITH PEOPLE WHO SHARE YOUR VALUES

The last line of George Orwell's *Animal Farm* is a stunner: "The creatures outside looked from pig to man, and from man to pig, and from pig to man again; but already it was impossible to say which was which."

You become your environment. If you associate with unethical people, you will become one of them. As you spend time with people, you will adopt their styles, values, and decision-making processes. You probably know this and apply it to the people you have hired for your team, but don't stop there. Include suppliers, your advertising agency—even your customers—on that list. Surround yourself with people of integrity and you will find your own storms easier to navigate.

GET INTO THE LIGHT

The state of Florida pioneered so-called sunshine laws that have been adopted by most state and local governments. "Sunshine" refers to the requirement that all government business be conducted in meetings open to the public and scrutiny of news media. Justice Louis Brandeis said, "Sunlight is the best disinfectant." It is difficult to proceed unethically when you are in the spotlight.

Adopt this method within your company; make it a part of your business's routine procedures. Unless dealing with confidential information, trade secrets, or sensitive personnel issues, involve as many people as possible in the process. If confidentiality prevents you from publicly airing an issue, always consider how the decision would be perceived if you were to take it public. The act of considering the public's reaction will often serve the same purpose as opening the meeting to the actual public.

MULTIPLY THE IMPACT

We often justify our actions by saying, "What's it going to hurt if I do it just once?" Whenever you catch yourself having this justification, imagine the impact if you did the contemplated action a hundred times. What would be the impact then?

VERBALIZE

I once decided the fate of a manager who had doctored employee time sheets, thus shortchanging the paychecks of minimum-wage workers. He was otherwise a good manager, and I decided he had acted so because of the strong pressure I had put on labor costs in the region. I told his supervisor not to fire him and, instead, take him within an inch of his life—have him apologize to the workers and reimburse them. I rationalized that he would learn from the mistake and be a stronger manager for it.

My boss reviewed the disciplinary memo I had issued and called me into his office. "Talk me through your thought process, Ken," was all he said. I began explaining my logic but stopped halfway through my second sentence. "I am absolutely wrong," I said, as I realized just how immoral my logic had been. No matter what the pressures, this man had violated a sacred trust and stolen from his workers. He had to be fired. There was no other possible decision. Yet, I had initially rendered a terrible decision, simply because I independently mulled it over in my own head.

Verbalizing the situation to others—it doesn't have to be your boss—will usually lead to the right decision on ethical issues. By having an open conversation, you share the risk, open the subject to diverse opinions, and force yourself to organize your thought process to the point that illogic is easily seen.

Use Your Brain

Sometimes ethical lines are crossed when we do stupid things. I once helped a man secure a nice position. His qualifications were powerful. For instance, he had two bachelor degrees to offer when the position did not even require one. After his employment, during a routine verification of his résumé, it was discovered that he did not have two degrees. He only had one. He was fired because he lied on his application. The company rationalized that if he was unethical enough to lie about something that didn't matter, what would he do when faced with an issue where it *did* matter? This individual's actions were both unethical and stupid. Routine use of basic brain cells would have avoided the problem.

Use Your Nose

A supplier, who has been doing business with your firm for ten years, begins offering you gifts of increasing value. An employee, who you have given a lot of well-deserved time off so he could help his sick wife, hands you tickets to a football game, just to say "thanks." Your boss casually mentions that if his wife should ask, you should tell her that you and he worked late at the office last Thursday night. Some situations carry an aroma. No matter how well rationalized, some options must be rejected because they flunk the smell test.

Use Your Heart

My first act as Benevolent Dictator will be to require all my subjects to watch an episode of *The Andy Griffith Show* each day. Here is one scene they will witness:

As Andy sat around the dinner table with Aunt Bee and Barney, his son Opie amused him with stories about a new friend, a magical man by the name of Mr. McBeevee. This amazing character had a shiny metal hat and made a jingling sound as he walked in the treetops. At first, the family laughed at Opie's imaginary friend but his Pa became worried as the stories grew more outrageous. After one evening of McBeevee stories, Barney and Aunt Bee confronted Andy and convinced him that he needed to put an end to the nonsense. Andy threatened Opie with a whippin' unless he declared that Mr. McBeevee was a work of fiction. Opie would not and was willing to accept the punishment. "I ain't lyin', Pa. Promise," Opie told his father. Andy retreated downstairs and stared into space. "Did you punish him?" Aunt Bee asks. "No," Andy quietly said. Barney was shocked at Andy's failure to act, "Don't tell me you believe in Mr. McBeevee!" "No," Andy replied. "But I do believe in Opie."

Andy's trust in Opie was rewarded the next day when he met Mr. McBeevee, who turned out to be a hard-hatted telephone lineman with a belt full of jingling tools. Sometimes, you have to toss all logic aside and let your heart declare the truth.

Frank was an excellent employee for many years, but began having attendance problems. He would arrive late several times a week, sometimes calling in sick (he was always "just feeling a bit under the weather"). Warnings and counseling attempts only had a temporary effect; after a few weeks, the problem would return. I eventually fired him. Frank's wife came to see me, and dragged Frank beside her. "Tell him!" she demanded. "Tell him your problem!" Frank hesitated and then blurted it out. He was an alcoholic. He wanted his job back and wanted help. I was under no legal obligation to do that. Also, all company rules had been followed, proper warning had been given, and all the right people had signed off on the termination. I had made the right decision and there was no legal or logical reason to reverse myself, but I did anyway. I chose to follow my heart. I had the power to change the man's life as well as retain an employee who could once again be a valuable company asset. Frank returned to employment, successfully fought his alcoholism, and became a symbol of hope for other employees with addictions.

Use Your Gut

Randy Cohen writes an ethics column for *The New York Times Magazine* (No, I'm not setting up an oxymoron here). His column fields ethical dilemmas from readers and dissects their problems. Most of the responses are predictable, but he has found a way to surprise me from time to time. For instance, he had no problem with smuggling food into a movie theater (although, he would not allow sneaking food into a restaurant). He is OK with letting a friend use your address to register her children in your better schools, since it is the government's responsibility to provide good schools and it is not the friend's fault that the city didn't do that in her district. He follows these statements with, frankly, impeccable logic.

There is one that has really amazed me. Cohen actually makes a convincing case for purchasing cheap seats at the ballpark, and then sneaking into unoccupied box seats when the usher is not looking. Readers who debated this declaration were shot down with crystal-clear, convincing logic. Now, I am not going to recount Mr. Cohen's argument here; I couldn't paraphrase his words in a manner that would do justice to his skillful logic. Cohen's analysis is indeed flawless.

I am a big fan of logical thinking, but I am certain that Cohen is absolutely wrong in his assertion that it is ethical to move into seats you didn't pay for. How can I be so sure I am right and this celebrated *New York Times Magazine* writer is dead wrong? His position just doesn't feel right; I know it in my gut.

Former New York Governor Mario Cuomo recalls: "Every time I've done something that doesn't feel right, it's ended up not being right." Your gut will tell you when it's the right decision. Good choices create a sense of peace. Choose that path.

Integrity is revealed in the small moments of our lives. The movie *Cinderella Man* is the story of a good, honorable man who maintains his dignity even under the most intense trials. Brilliantly played by Russell Crowe, Jim Braddock is a down-on-his-luck prizefighter trying to support his family during the Depression.

In one quiet, powerful scene that almost slips past us, Braddock walks outside to retrieve the milk delivery while his wife scrapes together a meager breakfast for their starving children. Braddock picks up an empty milk bottle and reads the note attached: "There will be no more milk until the bill is paid." The battered father looks around the nearby stairways and sees dozens of full milk bottles awaiting pickup by more fortunate neighbors. The alley is quiet. Braddock, alone with the snow and cold wind, surveys the gallons of nourishing milk. No one would miss just one bottle. No one would see what he did next. The next scene shows Braddock entering the house empty-handed. Integrity is what you do when no one is watching.

Some ethical decisions really are tough, but most are not. You can make immeasurable progress towards living an integrity-driven life by simply grabbing the obvious decisions and following your brain, nose, heart, and guts on the rest. Get the simple, routine daily decisions right and the complex ones will fall right into place.

There really is no such thing as an ethical team. Integrity is something only a human can demonstrate. Rather than trying to make your *company* ethical, just ensure each of your employees is a man or woman of integrity. Impart these principles to your team, one person at a time.

III

KEEPING YOUR TEAM

OK, I've taken that good advice on teambuilding and applied it to my beloved Braves. Looking back, I see a long list of great players we recruited and melded into an incredible team. Just look at this team!

Greg Maddux	Dale Murphy	Tom Glavine
Fred McGriff	Hank Aaron	Babe Ruth
Gary Sheffield	Eddie Mathews	Joe Torre

It's an amazing group! However, why aren't the Braves winning every single game they play with all these great players? It's because none of these men are Braves any longer. Some signed on with other teams, a couple retired, and a few just up and died. Whatever their reasons for leaving, these incredible players are no longer part of the team.

Yes, I'm really stretching to make my point here, but it does impart an important point. It doesn't matter how great a job you do recruiting or how great a team you build, all of that is a complete waste of time, effort, and cash if your wonderful team members leave your team.

Chances are you bought this book because the material about recruiting attracted you, or you wanted to ensure that you build a solid team. You probably weren't seeking retention advice. However, recognize this: Attrition is a slow-growing cancer. It attracts little attention in that early stage we call start-up. During this time, you search for answers to your immediate problems. Hiring and teambuilding are urgent; attrition can wait.

You will learn something in this section. You'll learn that turnover is costly—far more costly than you could have ever imagined. You'll learn that even though you have a revolutionary business idea, produce a high-quality product or service, and have surrounded yourself with a magnificent team, turnover will kill your dream.

However, as an entrepreneur you will look at all this horrid news a bit differently. You will have a more positive perspective. While your competitors are wallowing in the despair of attrition, you will celebrate the rewards of retention. Your job will be easier. Your company will grow. *Much* more cash will float to the bottom line. Retention will be your secret weapon.

11

The Real Cost of Attrition

The line grew until it was out the door and then halted just after it reached the sidewalk. It did not grow beyond that point, because potential customers drove away once they realized how long they would have to wait. Most only had thirty minutes for lunch and that time would expire before they could even place an order.

I was traveling to an out-of-state speaking engagement. Ahead of schedule, I decided to pull into a restaurant that was part of the same chain I once worked with. I arrived before the lunch rush began and was able to briefly chat with Roger, the manager. He mentioned that because he only had five people, the next ninety minutes would be difficult indeed. I asked him how many people he was supposed to have working. "Eleven" he said. "How will you handle it?" I asked. Roger explained that he would save four employees just by closing the drive-thru. (I happened to know that it would also cost him 59 percent of his sales, but chose not to fan his frustration.) "And the rest of the shortage, well, I dunno," he said. "I'll pre-make a whole bunch of burgers, that'll help some, and then we'll all work real hard like we always do."

I excused myself, grabbed a table, and pulled out some paperwork as I watched the drama unfold. I calculated that he did about $350 in sales, but let about $575 drive away. (My calculations did not include the thousands of future dollars he lost from unhappy customers who will never return.)

Lunch was over after about an hour-long frenzy. I resumed my conversation with the manager. "I have a terrible labor shortage," he said. "I'm authorized to have forty-three crew members and I've only got twenty. We've been open almost a year and that is all I have on my staff." He added the sentence that makes my ears turn red: "You just can't hire people around here."

"You've only been able to hire twenty people in a year?" I asked, knowing what his response would be. "Well, no," he replied. "Over the past year, I've probably hired about a hundred, but they just keep quitting on me."

I bit my tongue, choosing to leave him with some (normally, very expensive) business advice. "Roger, you don't have a hiring problem. You're *great* at hiring. What you have is a retention problem. Instead of continuously pouring more water in the bucket, you need to plug the holes in the bottom."

He looked at me just like my cocker spaniel did when I explained the string theory of quantum mechanics. I made one last feeble attempt to be of service. "How does this impact you financially?" I asked. His eyes lit up. "Oh that's the good part. Since people are so expensive, most of our bonus is tied to labor costs. I've saved so much in labor costs that I'll make a record bonus this quarter!"

I have read many articles and heard countless discussions about the costs of turnover. I've enjoyed these analyses and appreciated the point they all wanted to make: *Turnover is expensive.* Despite their good intentions, most analyses barely scratch the surface. They capture only the blatantly obvious—the actual checks written when an employee leaves the company. They include things like recruiting costs and training costs, but ignore other, real expenses like the loss of productivity, lowered reputation and morale, and lost customers. Perhaps some of these costs are tough to calculate, but they are very real expenses nonetheless. You have to work a bit at it, but you can absolutely convert a titanic list of turnover costs into cold tangible cash.

That is what we'll do in this chapter. We'll put the solution on hold for a few pages so we can gain a solid understanding of what it really costs for what is often perceived as a routine business event.

OUT-OF-POCKET COSTS

Let's first look at the more obvious costs incurred with turnover. These are the in-your-face costs that are easy to identify and calculate.

Exit Costs

Terminations can be messy. If involuntary, a termination may require the services of an attorney to construct a separation agreement or even deal with a threatened lawsuit. These separation agreements may include sizable severance payments, continuation of benefits, and even prorated bonuses. Also, consider the increase in your unemployment insurance rates, which are determined by your company's turnover experience.

Even voluntary resignations result in expensive baggage. Many benefits and bonuses may escalate, requiring immediate payoffs upon termination. Even with voluntary resignations, you are still exposed to the possibility of legal disputes, settlements, and judgments.

Recruitment Expenses

The cost to simply find a replacement is staggering. Here's a big one right up front: agency fees. A competent executive search firm will charge a minimum of 25 percent of the employee's estimated first-year's salary; 33 percent is more common. You are not much better off doing it yourself. You will find that the cost of advertising, brochures, and travel, added to the value of the time everyone—especially you—expends on working to fill the position, will come quite near this number. The time required for reference checks, testing, verification, and making travel arrangements is far more significant that you realize at first glance.

Perhaps your company is large enough that you actually have an in-house staff dedicated to recruiting, or one that recruits part-time. The time they spend replacing workers (as opposed to hiring due to expansion) is most certainly a recruitment expense as is the cost of all their benefits, office space, travel expenses, etc.

Relocation

The cost for moving an executive a modest distance can easily be $20,000. If you have to bridge any loss of equity in the house, $100,000 is not out of the question.

New Employee Salary

Because of salary compression (the phenomenon that workers' pay increases rarely keep up with the market rate), you will almost certainly need to pay the new worker more than the one leaving. Because this gap grows over time, this salary jump will be greater the longer the exiting employee was with your company. Expect this expense to increase 5 percent to 15 percent or much more if the exiting employee had been with you for a long time.

Equity Raises to Others

No matter how carefully you try to keep salaries confidential, they don't stay that way. Your new employee's paycheck will be headline news before the sun sets. You will quickly be bombarded with employee logic. *I've been with this company for three years and make x. He's been here fifteen minutes and makes x + 17 percent. That's not fair!* Listening to this barrage will eventually affect your decision making. Over the next year, your entire staff will see their salaries adjusted much higher than you would have done otherwise.

Also, the new salary you pay will become a benchmark for future hires, even at different pay levels. This is particularly troublesome if your business has plans for aggressive growth.

Signing Bonus

Once reserved exclusively for executives, signing bonuses have become more common. These one-time payments are used for a variety of reasons, including reimbursement for bonuses lost when leaving the old company, indirect moving expenses, or simply bridging a gap in salary negotiations.

In any event, their use will only increase over the next decade due to the insatiable demand for talent.

Training Costs

Direct training costs are significant, and we'll revisit this category when discussing the impact on your team and customers. For the moment, recognize the cost of salaries, etc., to anyone you have dedicated to training new employees. (Yes, trainers can be used for other purposes, such as developing existing employees. Consider this: if they do not have to train new employees, they can dedicate all their time to revenue-enhancing activities, such as developing existing employees.) Any time that an employee could spend on other productive projects should be calculated as direct costs of turnover.

Also include the cost of the employee while he is being trained. Do you have a six-week training program? That costs you another 11.5 percent of his total annual compensation. Does your training period last but a short week? Then it's "only" a hit of 2 percent. So, for a $50,000 employee (plus benefits), the cost of *just the training period alone* is at least $1,300 per week. Does the training include materials, programs to be purchased, travel? It all adds up quickly.

Replacement Labor

The job must get done even if the position is empty. Temps can be employed to fill some positions such as the receptionist, administrative assistant, or accountant positions, but temp fees are pricey. You may be able to avoid the expense of temporary workers by spreading the work among your other staff, but this is a short-term solution. As an entrepreneur, you would not have created the position if it were possible for your existing staff to handle it.

Many hourly positions, such as restaurant workers, mechanics, and stockkeepers, can be replaced by offering overtime to peers. While this may help with your business operations, the cost of overtime (150 percent, plus related taxes and fees) will make this an expensive option. All these options are so expensive that you may be forced to leave the work undone until the replacement is hired. That could be the most costly choice you make. (Not to pile it on, but think of the additional costs these solutions create: diminished quality from exhausted machinists working overtime, accounting errors from temps unfamiliar with your system, and lost sales due to clients being ignored.)

Paper Clips

Most new employees want or need new equipment and supplies, and you should include these items on this list. The list might include a set of tools or a supply of uniforms. It might include a new laptop (fortunately, most employees are willing to inherit a used desktop). You may need to redecorate an office or, at the very least, clean the mechanic's new work area. Even consider the cost of changing the locks on the door, putting a new nameplate on the desk, or printing new business cards. Individually, these expenses are small but you will be amazed at their impact when you add them up.

You can see how just these expenses can easily add up to one and one-half or two times of an employee's annual salary. Also note that these are just the *easily* quantifiable costs. We're about to see why I call those costs are just tips of the iceberg. They are easy to see but pale in comparison to the mass under the surface. Now let's look at underlying costs that, though not as easy to identify, may still have a colossal impact on your company.

IMPACT ON YOUR OPERATIONS

Decreased Productivity While Job Hunting

Your business suffers long before the resignation is submitted. The employee has been preoccupied with his job search for months, dedicating time to it rather than your business. Productivity has all but come to a halt during this period and both the quantity and quality of his work is diminished.

Loss of Expertise

The former employee had developed some expertise that cannot be duplicated. He knew the routines, other employees, and clients. That employee understood the business and may have even been sitting beside you as you pondered your dreams and created the business. The employee possessed lots of knowledge and expertise and, no matter how competent his replacement, these things cannot be fully recaptured.

Effect on Co-Workers

Co-workers know when a teammate is looking for a job and there is a strong impact on morale during this time. The grapevine is filled with updates, and gossip is constant. Conversations quickly warp into discussions about why he is leaving and then evolve into "I wonder if he'll know of a job for me?"

This impact is even stronger if the co-worker is their boss. One subject around the coffeepot will be, "Does he know something we don't know?" Consider the time wasted as employees begin to fret about who their new boss will be, followed by "Gee, the company had better promote one of us."

The Domino Effect

A termination makes your other employees vulnerable to pirating, not only from the ex-employee but headhunters as well. (When a resignation occurs, headhunters smell blood in the water and quickly begin to circle.) Frequent turnover brands your business as an easy source of potential labor; that reputation expands exponentially with each turnover. Turnover begets turnover.

Loss of Productivity

Productivity will suffer from the time the chair is vacated until the new guy is fully trained and up to speed. How long is this? Just filling the job is not enough. Even the time it takes to train is not the issue. The biggest problem may occur in the period between training completion and competent performance. For some, this process only takes a few weeks. For other positions—such as key management, research, or product development—it could take a year. This productivity gap could be the most expensive entry on this sad list.

Chaos

Some people are so essential to your company that their absence causes your operation to be frightful to run. "Lower productivity" is an inadequate description. Things more closely resemble hell on a bad day.

Your Focus

How does turnover affect your effectiveness? Realize that more is involved than just the time you have to spend finding a replacement or covering the workload yourself. Also calculate what you could have done with your time; for example, how many new clients could you have brought onboard?

IMPACT ON CUSTOMERS

Look beyond your four walls. The customer impact may have the most lasting effect on your business.

Diminished Quality

The quality of your product or service will decrease, at least until the employee is replaced and that employee becomes fully competent in the job. Customers burned during this time may never return.

Diminished Reputation

What is the value of your good name? What is the effect of a former employee saying bad things about you or your business?

Sales Loss

What happens when your salesperson leaves to go work for your competitor? More to the point, what happens to a lot of your customers when your salesperson goes to work for your competitor? This issue doesn't just apply to your sales force. You can also see it in professional firms such as physicians, accountants, insurance agents, and stockbrokers.

Permission

While I am sure you have developed a loyal customer base, every business has clients who are on the edge. Maybe they are not completely satisfied with your prices, quality, or service, but they haven't gotten around to looking elsewhere. The loss of their contact is often enough to cause their eyes to wander. Changing their representative gives your customers permission to shop around.

LOSS OF INTELLECTUAL CAPITAL

The cost of some turnover cannot be calculated because some employee knowledge cannot be duplicated. Lose them and their contributions are lost forever. Consider these losses:

Opportunity Costs

Losing a key person may put planned expansion on hold for a year or it might not even happen at all. Consider the effect of losing a research scientist or the manager of a long-term project? The project could be delayed years waiting for the new project manager to be brought up to speed or it could be abandoned completely.

Expertise

Some people cannot be replaced. They possess unique knowledge or skills that cannot be duplicated. Research scientists, athletes, and chefs are obvious examples.

However, your receptionist could also fall into this category. She may have an excellent relationship or deep knowledge about one of your key clients. Lose her and lose that relationship. The assistant who has been by your side since your business was a wee puppy is yet another example. Her knowledge about the details of your business cannot be replaced.

Loss of Company Secrets

The employee takes more than his nameplate when he leaves. He also takes your proprietary information, formulas, and recipes. No matter how sincere he may be, he cannot forget those things he learned while working for you.

LET'S CUT TO THE BOTTOM LINE

Many studies have attempted to value the cost of a single turnover. Because of the variables we have just seen, pegging an exact cost may be a purely academic exercise. However, their analyses provide some interesting issues to consider:

- The Society for Human Resource Management determined replacing an $8 per hour frontline employee (such as a restaurant worker) costs $3,500. This means that a typical fast-food restaurant employing 30 workers and experiencing a 100 percent annual turnover rate sees their bottom line reduced by an extra $100,000 per year. (Interesting fact: Seventeen organizations analyzed this scenario and SHRM's estimate was the lowest.)
- Here is another perspective I've reached by averaging estimates from several dozen analysts. Turnover costs you about 50 percent of the annual salary of entry-level employees, 150 percent of middle level employees, and up to 400 percent for specialized, high-level employees. If you have been keeping a running tally during the past few pages, you will know these estimates are conservative.
- Let's peer from yet another perspective. Let's say you turn five employees at an average replacement cost of only 1 × annual salary. To make the math easy, let's say their average salary is $50,000. We have a total loss of $250,000. This is cash that will not make it to your bottom line. What about the top line? Let's assume you run a profit margin of 10 percent. If so, then you need to generate an additional $2,500,000 in revenue just to cover the loss of these five employees.

WHY THIS MATTERS TO YOU

I've just presented you with some case studies from giant companies, cited money amounts into the tens of millions, and referred to global statistics. However, your have a small company with humble revenue and may not even do business outside the city limits of Racine. You may have a problem relating to this discussion and perhaps feel like it is a problem that only big corporations must be bothered with.

Let me assure you that this discussion is indeed focused directly toward you. Turnover has an even greater effect on your business than it has on MegaGlobal. Look at the discussion on the impact of losing a salesperson. We showed how this loss can impact customer relations, disrupt marketing efforts, and even lead to a loss of that person's clients. The impact of losing a single salesperson can be devastating to a giant international company.

While losing one salesperson (out of a hundred) is certainly a blow to big companies, they are so big that they can absorb the consequences. How about you? In all probability, you only have one salesperson and losing him actually means you have lost your entire sales force!

As we have quantified, MegaGlobal does indeed suffer losses when a single worker quits, but at least they can easily spread the work among his peers. Other mechanics can pick up the slack. Managers can be shuffled between stores. Factory workers can pick up a little overtime. However, when *you* lose a manager, mechanic, or machine operator, chances are strong that they are the only one you had. Work will come to a halt until their replacement is found and gets up to speed. Losing a single worker is painful to a giant corporation. For you, it could be fatal.

MAKING LEMONADE

This chapter has taken quite a negative approach, hasn't it? I wrote it that way to grab your attention, but let's switch to a different tack. Being an entrepreneur, your DNA is programmed to see opportunity in every disaster, and this is no exception. Instead of further hammering on with the harm of heavy attrition, let's look at the amazing benefits of reducing employee turnover.

While it is true that a $50,000 per year employee who resigns costs you about $150,000 on your bottom line (assuming a 3 × impact), it is also a fact that saving a $50,000 per year employee eliminates $150,000 in costs—that $150,000 cost savings floats unobstructed to your bottom line. Is this hypothetical money, phantom money, theoretical money? No; It is no more theoretical than saving $150,000 on any other cost is "theoretical" cash. If your annual cost for supplies was $5,000,000, and you found a vendor who could deliver the supplies for 3 percent less, that $150,000 savings wouldn't be the least bit theoretical, would it?

The Small Business Administration estimates that if you reduce turnover by 15 percent, you will increase your profit by 25 percent. Read that sentence again. *Drop turnover by 15 percent, increase profit by 25 percent*. What other actions could you take that would have such an incredible impact on your profitability? Also, what would those actions cost?

Note another implication of this analysis: You don't have to have a huge turnover problem in order to capture these benefits. Even if your turnover is modest, even if you are the envy of your industry, dropping your turnover by just 15 percent will land another 25 percent on your bottom line. This discussion is not only for the companies in crisis; it is just as beneficial to those with healthy performances.

As a business owner, you must regularly evaluate how you allocate your time and money in order to receive the best return. There is no better place to invest your assets than in employee retention.

THE REST OF THE STORY

I bumped into a former employee about a year after my experience with Roger. I was pleased to learn that he was now a franchise consultant for our old company. Coincidentally, he oversaw the territory that included Roger's restaurant. I asked how that store was doing. "The franchisee closed it about two months ago," he said. "It's a shame, really, but sales were just too low. I guess it was just a lousy market for us." Some companies suffer sizable cash losses due to turnover. Others are distracted by the inconvenience. However, for this franchisee, the cost was total. He lost his business.

12

The Four Pillars of Retention

In Chapter 11, we explored the incredible devastation turnover can have on business as well as the competitive advantages you can receive when you improve retention. Perhaps the most telling statistic presented was that the SBA declared that a 15 percent improvement in turnover will yield a 25 percent increase in your profit.

I work with several accounting firms as they assist their clients in uncovering ways to save or make money. Obviously, employee turnover offers incredible opportunities for these companies; they always benefit dramatically when they convert these theories into cash.

Here are two good questions I am always asked: "OK Ken, even if this is so, even if I can get a 25 percent profit increase by decreasing turnover by 15 percent, what does it cost me to get that 15 percent? And how do I do it?" The answer to the first question is very little—often, nothing at all. The answer to the second question is: You will achieve these results by incorporating the *four pillars of retention*. They are:

- Find a need and fill it.
- Match the employee with the right job.
- Provide a good boss.
- Develop a culture of retention.

PILLAR 1: FIND A NEED AND FILL IT

When you became an entrepreneur, your first decision was to determine the type of business you would create. The most oft-cited you heard was: *Find a need and fill it*. That is also the solution to turnover. Find out what the employee needs and provide that need. That's it. If you promise to follow that advice, you can now dispense with the rest of this book and go walk the dog.

OK, maybe that's vague. That instruction was like the seminar Steve Martin presented called *How to Own a Million Dollars in Real Estate in Two Easy Steps*. Step one: Get a hold of a million dollars. (I told this story to a real estate investor. He disagreed. "The best way to own a million dollars in real estate is to buy *two* million dollars worth of real estate," he explained.)

While that statement was too brief, the attrition solution really is that simple. People work because they have needs. They accepted your job because they felt you were their best chance to have those needs met. They will continue to be on your team as long as they feel you continue to meet their needs. They will leave your company when they feel someone else will better meet their needs.

You know this instinctively. While you may not have thought of it in those terms, you packaged your job offer (including title, scope, compensation, and other features) in such a manner that you felt it would attract the best candidates. No matter how you parse the subject, that was your attempt to meet the employee's needs.

The Golden Rule

We use this same approach as we try to retain our team. We want to remain their first choice for this need-meeting. (Sorry about the technical terminology.) This is often where the manager gets into trouble. We meet needs that don't exist while ignoring those that do. Do you know who messes up the worst at this? It is the well-intentioned manager—the one who is the most people-focused and caring. He messes up because he wants to do the right thing. He messes up because he follows the golden rule.

Before burning me at the stake, let's look at what the golden rule says: *Do unto others as you would have them do unto you.* Do you see the problem with that statement? Look at this example:

> Geof is excited with his promotion to division director. He is proud of his achievement and eager to show the world why he was given such a prestigious position at a young age. His first big problem is that David the accountant, Lynn the receptionist, and Doris the advertising guru are all rumored to be looking elsewhere. Geof wants to keep them, of course, so he takes action. He asks himself, "What would motivate me to stay?" Since Geof is personally motivated by prestige, he changes their titles. David is now Senior Accountant, Lynn becomes Visitor Relations Manager, and Doris is the new Marketing Manager. He also gives them spiffy new business cards announcing their new status. Within a month, David has gone to work for a company that promised to pay for his master's degree. Lynn has a job with work hours that make it easier to shuttle her kids to day care. Doris got a nice pay raise when she accepted the advertising coordinator's job with a competitor.

While cloaked in the best of intentions, Geof's mistake was that he didn't meet their needs. He addressed his own. For the purposes of retention, we need to tweak the golden rule, and change it to: *Do unto others the way they want to be done unto.*

How Do They Want to Be Done Unto?

You keep people by meeting *their* needs. In order to do this, we must first know what their needs are. To further complicate the problem, realize that those needs are in constant flux. People want different things at different times of their lives. They may be initially focused on compensation, later crave job security, and then want to expand the scope of their job. Later, they may crave power, prestige, or influence. No matter how sincere you are, you can't meet each employee's needs if you don't know what those needs are.

How do you find out what each employee needs? You ask. You ask *the question* I have touted throughout this text: If you were to leave this company and go to work somewhere else, what would probably be the reason? The employee's answer to this question is the need that needs to be met.

Make use of this tool throughout the employee's career. Here is how:

- When the employee first joins your team, ask him, "What made you decide to come to work here?" His answer will tell you his initial motivation. Record it in his file.
- Ask the same question about once a month for the first few months. Then follow this by asking him, "Are we meeting that expectation?" Again, keep the answers on file.
- Throughout the employee's tenure, frequently ask *the question*: If you were to leave this company and go to work somewhere else, what would probably be the reason? (As you manage by wandering around and record the answer in his file).
- Certainly ask *the question* during the annual review process. Again, follow up by asking the employee how you are doing in that area. For instance, if the employee responds "to have a job with more responsibility," consider expanding the scope of her job. Ask her to describe the new responsibilities she would like to take on. Design a personal development program that provides the education, training, and tools she needs to perform the additional functions. In other words, *fill the need*.

Interpreting the Employee's Answer

You can usually take the employee's response at face value. You ask the question and she tells you her current need. However, sometimes the response may need to be analyzed more closely. Here are some examples:

A Vague Response.   Make sure you understand what the employee is stating. The first utterances to an unexpected inquiry might be broad or unfocused. Let the employee talk and draw her answer out. What does she mean if she says, "to take care of my kids"? Is your health insurance plan adequate? Perhaps she wants to stay at home with them full-time. Maybe she just needs her schedule tweaked so she is not so rushed when she drops them off at day care. Don't let her answer float in uncertainty; get clarification.

No Response. The employee may have no answer. He might say, "Hmmm, let me think about that. I really don't know." This is a fine response. It indicates there really aren't any major unaddressed needs and the employee hasn't considered other employment.

Long Pause, Then a Cliché. After the employee has pondered for a moment, he responds, "Gosh, I don't know ... more money?" Interpret this just as you did the non-response. The employee hasn't thought about it but figures you need an answer, so she grabbed an obvious one.

Long Pause, Then a Thoughtful Answer. This is the best response; you can really work with this information. There has been a long pause because the employee really hasn't thought about it. She is satisfied with her job and is not "on the market." However, when she thinks about it, she is sincerely considering the next stage of her life. Pay careful attention to her eventual response. We'll use the previous example and assume she says, "I would probably be looking for a job where I had more responsibility." Drop everything you are doing and immediately pull her into your office and put together a development plan. You'll catch her unmet need before it becomes an unmet need.

A Quick, Forceful Response. As they sing in *The Music Man,* "Oh we got trouble, Right here in River City!" An immediate response means he's been thinking about this very issue. The forceful response means she's mad about it. There is a major need you are not meeting; she may already be looking for another job. Quick forceful responses require quick forceful action. You must have an immediate, candid discussion and work hard if you want to keep this employee.

Eating an Elephant

There is a serious flaw with Pillar 1. Pillar 1 states that if you meet your employees' needs, they will stay; if you don't meet their needs, they'll leave. Here is the flaw: The statement is expressed in the plural. Your sincere efforts will fail if you take the statement literally. That is because it is not possible to meet your employees' needs; in fact, there is no such thing as "the employees' needs." There are only individual needs. Employees can only be saved one at a time.

Now this distinction is not an academic one. Companies make this mistake often, even with the best of intentions. Most companies conduct annual culture surveys hoping to measure the team's level of satisfaction. Scores will be tallied and management will determine the areas it can work on to make their employees happier. Understand that I am not mocking this process. I make a very good living conducting these surveys. Indeed, the culture survey has many excellent applications; it's just that uncovering employee needs is not one of them.

Yes, there may be general dissatisfaction with the color of the lunchroom, the clarity of communications, or even the level of benefits. These are certainly issues that management will want to look at. However, these are not issues that will cause any one individual to leave the company and go to work elsewhere. Culture surveys do measure general satisfaction levels but they do not reflect retention issues.

Employees cannot be retained as a group. They must be addressed as individuals with distinct individual needs. Address those individual needs and you will keep your team members.

PILLAR 2: MATCH THE EMPLOYEE WITH THE RIGHT JOB

Job mismatch is the number one cause of voluntary turnover, the number one cause of involuntary turnover, the biggest cause of job burnout, and the major reason so many people hate their jobs. Selecting the wrong career field will doom a person to a lifetime of misery and mediocrity. It is that serious.

So, perhaps you will find it a bit surprising that I use Michael Jordan to illustrate my point; Yes, *that* Michael Jordan—the greatest basketball player in history and the one that all other books use to illustrate success.

I had the good fortune to follow Michael Jordan's career during a year I lived in Birmingham. During that year, he retired from basketball and decided to take up *baseball* playing right field for a minor league affiliate of the Chicago White Sox.

Understand that Michael displayed his amazing character during that year. His charisma was infective. He was respectful of his coaches and teammates, generous to the fans, and spent a tremendous amount of his time with the kids and local charities. As a man he was extraordinary, but as a baseball player he was average. His fielding was acceptable. He had a batting average a bit below average and he hit only one home run the entire season. Michael Jordan, despite his hard work, amazing attitude, and legendary determination, never made it to the major leagues. Michael Jordan wasn't good enough.

Ponder that statement. Michael Jordan, the greatest basketball player who has ever lived, wasn't good enough to make a major league baseball roster. No one ever dominated any sport the way he dominated basketball. Yet, even Michael Jordan was unable to transfer those talents to a relatively similar career. The consequences of job mismatch are that significant. If Michael Jordan was unable to overcome the disaster of job mismatch, how do you think Harry the salesman or Sarah the schoolteacher will do?

Subtle mismatches are far more dangerous than obvious ones. Obvious mismatches will be disasters from day one as the job explodes in the person's face. Donald Trump would immediately learn he should not have become a plumber. Any employer would quickly recognize that Robin Williams should not have been hired as an actuary. Paris Hilton would be exposed as a fraud if she, well, if she did almost anything.

Obvious job mismatches loudly announce their presence and quickly exit the building. However, a subtle mismatch is a slow march toward hell. Think what would have happened if Michael had initially chosen a baseball career rather than basketball. Yes, he would have been good enough to be signed to a minor league contract. However, he would have spent several years just plugging along in the minor leagues, always just good enough to stay on a roster but never quite good enough to make the big leagues. If he had finally reached the major leagues, his career would have certainly been short and forgettable. He would have struggled along until he was unceremoniously released, then taken a job selling appliances, delivering freight, or maybe even becoming a high school coach. (I am not dissing these occupations. There is nothing wrong with these careers. They can be wonderful careers *if* that is where your talents and passions lie.)

That is the horror of subtle job mismatches. You are able to keep your head above water only because you work hard and are somewhat in your element. You are just good enough that you blame your mediocrity on your job rather than your profession. So you spend that career moving from company to company, by your choice and theirs, never having that explosive moment that kicks you into your true calling. (Homework assignment: Rent the movie *The Death of a Salesman*. It captures the frustration, loneliness, and eventual tragedy that come from working in a job that is almost, but not quite, the right match. Then, offer Willie Loman some specific career advice. My suggestions can be found on my Web site, www.kentanner. net.)

How Do You Ensure Job Match?

We'll never completely solve the problem. Even if we could come up with a sure-fire system for guaranteeing everyone landed in their ideal career field, we would then face the reality that people change. How's that? Think of what you always wanted to be "when you grew up." Did that change? (Of course it did. Otherwise, the workforce would be composed of nothing but firefighters, cowboys, and runway models.) Now, compare the career options that filled your passions and talents when you were nineteen (when you chose your college major) with the desires you have today. Job match is a moving target and that makes this already frustrating subject even more of a challenge.

Take a Deep Breath

The biggest checkpoint is, of course, during the hiring process. Both the candidate and the employer must share the blame for haphazard hiring practices—decisions often colored by urgent situations.

Too many job seekers take the first job they are offered. This is understandable, especially if the candidate is unemployed and eager to change that status. When the rent is overdue, you will easily convince yourself that you have always wanted to be a used futon salesman. Likewise, when the zookeeper position has been unfilled for weeks and alligators are eyeing your customers, the former hairstylist in your lobby starts looking pretty good. Many job mismatches can be avoided if everyone would just show a bit more patience.

Test for Subtleties

Consider using one of many excellent vocation tests in the hiring process. These are especially useful in uncovering subtle mismatches. For example, an Ohio trucking company used a testing program to uncover some issues with drivers. They found that while all of their team was well suited to the general umbrella of driving trucks, there were subtle differences between those who delivered in-town versus those carrying interstate cargo. Testing showed two distinct personality types and they reassigned the drivers based on those types. In-town routes with lots of customer interaction were given to those drivers with bubbly people skills. The solitary, socially challenged personalities were placed on the long-haul routes. Turnover dropped from 116 percent to 22 percent and the customers were a lot happier, too.

Hit the Moving Target

Pay close attention to the next chapters as we discuss filling employee needs. We'll explore how to discover those ever-changing needs and ways to address those needs as they evolve. This might require training, movement to new positions within your company, or maybe just a little rewriting of the job description. Regardless of the method used, you will have a better chance at retaining your employees if you are regularly seeking ways to design their jobs to best fit their needs.

PILLAR 3: PROVIDE A GOOD BOSS

Here is an accepted HR principle: *People join companies and leave managers*. Unquestionably bad managers will run off the good employees you have worked so hard to attract, but what is it about a boss that makes him "bad"? What are the specific character traits that cause an employee to quit? What would a boss have to do, say, or be that would be enough to directly motivate an employee to leave an otherwise good job? The answer is that the manager is rarely the *direct* reason for the resignation. Sure, we've all heard stories about mean bosses, incompetent bosses, and harassing bosses, but even the exaggerated tyrants caricatured on TV are rarely, by themselves, sufficient reason for a person to abandon his livelihood. We have all worked for yellers and screamers, nitpickers and slave drivers. Indeed, not only did they not drive us off, we often think of them to be the best bosses we ever had! So what are the reasons bad bosses have such outrageous turnover? In fact, what is it that makes a bad boss a bad boss?

My conclusion is that bad bosses lose people because they are not approachable. No matter how great his other flaws may be, a manager will retain his people if the employees feel comfortable talking with him about their issues.

Here is what I mean: Throughout their careers, all employees will have situations that cause them to consider leaving their jobs. Some examples are the need for a different work schedule to take care of their kids; the opportunity to go back to school; the need to pick up some overtime so they can generate a bit more cash; discouragement over their job performance; domestic issues causing a temporary reduction in productivity; a call from a headhunter; and the list goes on and on. It is during these times that people are susceptible to quitting and looking for "something else" or "somewhere else." Good managers are good problem solvers and the employee can be saved if he feels comfortable approaching his boss and discussing his problem while the issue is still minor. However, a turnover is guaranteed if the employee is afraid of his manager and allows the issue to fester into a major crisis.

How do you identify an unapproachable manager? Here's some circular logic for you: An unapproachable manager is one with a record of high turnover. They are isolated, uninformed, and unaware; they won't handle employee issues until they explode behind their backs. How do you develop your managers' approachability? Here are a few places to start:

- Hire managers with a record of retention.
- Only promote people who exhibit openness and approachability.
- Require your managers to regularly meet with employees one-on-one. This venue may prompt *oh-by-the-way* comments that will open the door for the employee to mention a developing issue.
- Encourage managers to leave their doors open. A closed door is more than a metaphor; employees feel alienated and cut off by physical barriers.
- Managers should make greetings more than a boilerplate gesture. "How are you?" can sometimes be the opening an employee needs to open up. Make sure managers don't kill the messenger. When people fear bringing you bad news, they'll soon avoid bringing you any news at all. On the other hand, if they see that you react maturely with bad news, they will feel they can talk to you about their own personal issues.

PILLAR 4: DEVELOP A CULTURE OF RETENTION

You will see retention rates soar when you and your entire team genuinely adopt an attitude insisting on tenure. Here are some ways to make it a part of your company's culture:

Acceptable Turnover

You must develop a mindset that turnover is completely unacceptable in your company. Is this realistic? No, turnover will occur, but so will theft, unhappy customers, and product errors. Do we tell our managers that we discourage stealing, but that it's OK as long as they don't take more than 15 percent of the cash? Even though we know some shrinkage is inevitable, we still set up zero tolerance systems. We do this because we know there is no stopping point once we start saying "Yes, but."

We must have the same mindset with turnover that we have with product defects, customer complaints, and employee thefts. Just as in those examples, we must firmly implant this mindset in every manager. How do we do this? How can we get our managers to take complete accountability for employee retention? There is a little game I play at my retention workshops. I will make this statement: "With five exceptions, any turnover can be traced back to a mistake made by the company at some point in that employee's relationship with the company. Just five. Let's see if we can identify those five situations."

The participants will describe situations, provide examples of people who have quit or were fired, and state how the manager was certain there was nothing the company could have done about it at any point in the process. Invariably, the first example will involve firing an employee who has stolen money. "You're not telling us that we can't fire thieves, are you?" they will say.

No, of course I'm not. A thief must be fired (with great vigor, I might add). You cannot tolerate dishonesty. Still, that does not mean that there was not a failure in the system at some point. How's that? Whenever you fire someone for stealing, first look at your recruiting process. People maintain their basic personalities throughout their lives. If she stole from you, then she stole from her previous employers. Did we do a proper reference check before bringing her onboard? Could a criminal background check have uncovered past indiscretions? Beyond that, are cash handling and auditing procedures adequate and firmly enforced? Perhaps the mistake the company made was in giving the employee the opportunity to steal. Yes, an employee who steals must absolutely be fired. Morally, it is unquestionably the employee's fault for doing what she did. However, that is not the question. The question is: Did the company have any control over this termination? The answer is yes.

A few more situations similar to this, such as sexual harassment or rudeness to a customer will be offered and my response will be similar: Check out the company's hiring procedures and operational safeguards.

Another manager will ask about firing a poor performer. "He tried hard, but he just couldn't hack it," he'll explain. By this time most of the audience will have absorbed the rationale. Two or three participants will battle for the honor of explaining that the company fell short in the recruiting and verification processes, as well as probably not having an effective training program.

Acceptable Reason 1: Death

A moment of silence will follow. And then a light bulb will appear over one participant's head. "How about *death*?" she will announce. "There's nothing the company could have done if an employee dies!"

"Yes, you have identified Acceptable Reason 1," I'll confirm. "Unless, of course, the employee died from a work-related injury."

What are the other four reasons? Under what circumstances can you blamelessly lose an employee? Here is the rest of the list:

Acceptable Reason 2: Personal Issues That Require Transfer out of the Area

The best example of this would be a spouse who is transferred out of state, but there are other situations that fit. For instance, I once had a manager whose child developed leukemia. The employee needed to move to Memphis where the little girl had been accepted into one of the miracle programs at St. Jude Children's Hospital. This was certainly an acceptable turnover.

Acceptable Reason 3: A Personal Growth Opportunity You Cannot Address

People grow and your small company may not always be able to address their dreams. Here are some examples: He might have been a line cook while getting his marketing degree, but is now accepting a job with a New York advertising agency; or she wants to become a full-time mom. Maybe she wants to serve the country and join the military, or a situation some of my clients frequently face, an employee feels called into the ministry. (What do you do in this situation? Nothing. Do not compete with God.) There are many situations where the employee wants to go down a path you cannot provide. Wish them well and take pride in the role you had in helping them along their journey.

Acceptable Reason 4: Salary Increase above 25 Percent

True, salary is something that you exercise control over, but there is a point where an employee may legitimately become too expensive for your company. Not only can you accept this turnover, but you can also be proud of your role in his development. Celebrate this advancement. (Unless, Ebenezer, you have been horridly underpaying him for all this time.)

Acceptable Reason 5: Extortion

This list originally had just four reasons. However, in July 2006, a South African company asked me to help them lower their attrition rates. As we reviewed each of their recent turnovers, I asked about an engineer who had been pirated by a nearby competitor. "Yeah, we really hated to lose him," the HR director said. "But their recruiter told him if he did not accept the offer they would kill his brother." And that is when I created this fifth category of acceptable turnover.

You Are Naïve, Ken

You probably question the commitment to zero turnover. For one thing, there are some benefits to some turnover, right? Without turnover, you will accept mediocre performance and it will be hard to achieve the lofty goals you have set for your enterprise. Besides, an organization without turnover soon becomes complacent and stagnates, but most of all, zero turnover is simply unachievable. It's naïve to set goals that cannot be achieved.

Agreed, I have often said many naïve things in my life, but this is not one of them. Your business will be stronger and have a greater chance of success if you declare no tolerance for attrition. Let's address some of those objections I hear when I make that statement.

Is zero turnover achievable? No, it is not. If nothing else, people die. Don't use statistics to determine your goals. The fact is your actual turnover will drop significantly just by being determined to eliminate it altogether. A culture of zero turnover will spur actions and attention that will in itself eliminate many losses. Even it you adopt this culture, even if you elevate it to a near religious fervor, you will still lose people. However, as you have seen from other unreachable goals, striving for their achievement still delivers exceptional results. If your turnover is currently 20 percent and you take it up as a cause, you'll at least cut it in half. That, as we have seen, will have an amazing impact on your business.

That also addresses the worry about zero turnover causing your company to stagnate. Make lemonade out of that 10 percent failure rate by using it to address stagnation and mediocre performers. I know I have just combined lofty idealism with cold realities, but let me address the issue of my "theories" being naïve. You are being naïve if you think you will ever achieve such a low attrition rate that you will have to worry about stagnation or retaining a poor workforce.

However, let's talk about the possible conflict between adopting a culture of retention and the reality of dealing with poor performers. Does this proposed culture encourage an acceptance of mediocrity? No, absolutely not. You should never accept poor performance for any reason. Poor performers must be cast from the system. Instead of having your initial response be to fire all poor performers, I am suggesting that your first instinct be to *turn them into good performers*.

Example: Let's assume four workers aren't hacking it. Non-performers must be removed from your business. If you take an arbitrary approach, you'll achieve this by firing four people. However, if you maintain a culture of retention, you'll do everything within reason to turn them into solid performers. Let's say you bat .500 by saving two of them and releasing the other two. In both systems, you have eliminated all the poor performers. With my system, you have half the number of people to terminate. (Does it cost a lot to save these two workers? Possibly, but compare it to the costs we uncovered in Chapter 11.)

Yes, it is true that a churn-free workforce will become stagnant. Without some turnover, new blood and new perspectives cannot enter the system.

Focus: *Does Attrition Become Less of an Issue When Unemployment Rates Are High?*

While the general long-term trend points to massive labor shortages, there will be *industries* that cycle through periods of high unemployment. You may be tempted to relax your retention efforts during these times, feeling that your employees won't be searching for greener pastures since so few jobs are available. That would be a mistake.

Yes, it is true that during tough economic times the *average* employee will not be able to find a better job. However, your *outstanding* ones will. The average performer is indeed stuck with you. Because there is always room at the top, good employees can easily find another job.

When jobs are scarce, the only people you have to worry about losing are your very best performers. That's not much comfort, is it? No matter what the economy or job market, focus on employee retention.

(Also, there is no better time to recruit than during a time when jobs are scarce. Go after that super employee you've had your eye on. Chances are he is feeling a bit insecure and will be quite receptive to your approach.)

Take another look at the Acceptable Turnover list. I assure you that you will have enough of these that stagnation will never be a problem in your life.

PERFORM THE AUTOPSY

You want to learn from your mistakes so you can improve future performance. That applies to turnover. Finding out where you went wrong will help decrease future attrition. You must uncover the real reason for the turnover. That reason is rarely the one she has given you. Exit interviews are meaningless and letters of resignation are worth even less. Since the employee won't tell you, you must find the cause yourself. Time for an autopsy.

Anytime you lose an employee, gather your team in a room, close the door, and have a good honest discussion. Examine the facts and records and listen to all opinions and insight. After enough discussion, the true cause of the turnover will become apparent. Perhaps you'll find a hole in your training process or the selection process. Maybe it was a lousy job match from the beginning or perhaps you are unaware of the presence of an office bully.

Then again, you may find that the termination stemmed from one of the five acceptable reasons we just reviewed. Just make sure it really is one of those reasons. Don't stretch the situation or use these to conveniently ignore real issues. Yes, the employee may have decided to change career fields, but are you sure she did so because she wanted to become a church secretary? Could there have been an office bully harassing her? Be brutally honest during the autopsy or you will send yourself down a path of fantasy.

Here is an exercise I often use in my retention workshops: Perform an autopsy on Johnny Paycheck. We'll listen to his lovely ballad *Take This Job and Shove It* and determine the real reason for his unexpected resignation.

We think we've discovered the reason in the very first verse when Johnny declares that his woman done left him and took all his money. Most managers will end the discussion right there upon hearing his explanation. The manager would realize that Johnny was having family problems, declare it inappropriate to become involved in personal issues, and show Johnny the door. The manager would be sorry to see him go, but relieved that it wasn't his fault and assume there was really nothing the company could do about it anyway.

However, one member of our autopsy team will realize there is something odd with the reason Johnny gave. If his wife ran off with all his money, why would he cut off his only income stream? Instead of quitting, he should be asking for more overtime!

So, we keep listening, allowing Mr. Paycheck to express himself poetically (well, at least the words rhyme) until—*aha!*—Johnny mentions something new. He says that while his foreman is a regular dog, the line boss (the one with a flat top haircut) thinks he is cool but is actually a fool. That's it! The real reason for the turnover has been revealed. This fifteen-year veteran is not quitting for "family reasons." He's quitting because his boss is a jerk. Now that we know what the real problem is, we just might be able to solve it. By performing an autopsy, we may be able to continue sending paychecks to Johnny.

The purpose of the autopsy is to find out what happened, make appropriate changes, and lessen the possibility of future turnovers. As with all problem-solving, you can't fix a problem until you have truly defined it. The autopsy process helps you uncover your actual problems. Conduct autopsies on all your resignations and attrition will steadily decline.

ONE AT A TIME

Field of Dreams is a chick flick for guys. Seriously, few men can watch it without shedding a few manly tears. Ray, an Iowa farmer, builds a baseball field in the spot where he should be growing corn. He does this because, as we all know, if you build a regulation baseball field in the middle of nowhere, the ghosts of great baseball players will appear.

Amazingly, that is exactly what happens. A stunned Shoeless Joe Jackson is the first to appear. After the boys play catch and bat some balls, Shoeless Joe decides to go tell the others. As he runs through the outfield to make his exit, he pauses and shouts a question to Ray. "Hey! Is this heaven?" he asks. "No," Ray replies. "It's Iowa."

Few people would confuse Iowa with heaven, but it is easy to see how Shoeless Joe Jackson would. By meeting his needs, this bald patch in a cornfield becomes the most wonderful place Shoeless Joe could imagine. Ray was wrong. For this one person, it *was* heaven.

Your business may not offer all the glitz MegaGlobal has. While they may have the assets to provide grand gleaming things for their employees *in general*, you are in the wonderful position to care for each employee's *individual* needs. Address each person, one-on-one, and do your best to meet their needs. As we will explore in the following chapters, you will have the advantage over the cold towering competitors.

Filling Job Needs

At the beginning of Chapter 12, we recognized the very first pillar of retention was to meet your employees' needs. What are we talking about when we refer to needs? I've based my retention approach on a needs theory you probably encountered in your freshman psychology class. Abraham Maslow's *Hierarchy of Needs* provides a solid foundation for recognizing what our employees need from their jobs.

Maslow's famous theory grew from his experiments with monkeys. By watching them, the idea began to gel that different needs take precedence over others. In fact, we don't move to a higher level until each preceding level is satisfied. Further, if you have attained a higher level and the lower level is suddenly taken away, your focus then falls completely to the level of the lowest unmet needs.

Let's return to Maslow's monkeys for a moment. He noticed that if a monkey was both hungry and thirsty, the monkey would first look to quench his thirst. (You can live without food for a few weeks, but can go without water only a couple of days.) Water is a more basic need, so the monkey addresses it before food. Once thirst is quenched, then hunger is satisfied, the monkey will move on to other desires/needs, such as playing or sex. However, if another monkey tries to choke him, the monkey will forget all other needs in an attempt to breathe. At that point, all other needs vanish and oxygen is all that matters.

Maslow developed his theory from all this monkey-watching. He soon moved from monkeys to people and created a ranking of our needs and wants. Here is how we stack up on his needs-pyramid:

1. *Physiological.* These are the most basic requirements to sustain human life: air, water, food, and shelter. (You may find this of interest: Maslow believed that a lack of vitamin C, for example, would lead to a specific hunger for things that contained vitamin C, such as fruit or juice.)
2. *Security.* Once physiological needs are provided, your focus shifts to assuring your safety and security. You also need to address your fears and anxieties.

3. *Social.* When the first two levels are met, humans then develop a strong urge for friends, a mate, and a family. At this point, loneliness and isolation will cause severe harm and a well-balanced person has a strong need for community.
4. *Esteem.* Now we move into the higher levels of human needs. While we can live without these things, it is important for most people to experience factors that separate him from the lower species. These include respect, status, fame, glory, recognition, appreciation, and dignity.
5. *Self-actualization.* We have now reached the mountaintop. According to Maslow, once all the other levels have been satisfied, humans want to accomplish something special in their lives. As they say in the Army commercials, you want to "Be all you can be."

As you were reading this brief psychological primer, you undoubtedly saw where I was headed. Those life-needs can be easily transferred to things people want from their careers. Indeed, I do base my retention system on Maslow's *Hierarchy of Needs*. Consider this: The U.S. Department of Labor asked workers what they most wanted from their jobs. Their responses correlate, *in exact order*, with Maslow's theory. Here is how it all adds up:

Uncle Sam	Maslow
Challenging job	Self-actualization
Recognition, feeling valued	Esteem
Friendships, good relationships	Social needs
Job security	Security
Money, benefits	Physiological

You just can't ignore this alignment of social theory and government statistics. Thus, we will spend the next two chapters looking at these employee needs and discussing turnover solutions based on meeting those needs. In this chapter, we will focus on basic needs, those that an employee must have in order to simply function in a job: compensation and security are absolutes. The employee will most certainly leave your company if these basic needs are not met. I refer to these as "job" needs.

In the next chapter we will address "career" needs. By having these needs met, an employee begins to rise from just having a job to developing a rewarding career. Unmet needs in these areas—social, esteem, and actualization—will not necessarily cause the employee to walk out the door, but will make her increasingly vulnerable to seeking greener pastures.

But before I use any more animal metaphors, let's explore the employee's most basic needs. We must begin with money.

A SOLID COMPENSATION PACKAGE

Here is a telling scene from the TV show *Desperate Housewives*: The self-centered diva Gabrielle sums up many people's attitudes toward money during an argument with her husband. When Carlos points out that "money doesn't buy happiness," she replies, "Oh, of course it does. That's just something we tell poor people to keep them from rioting."

The role of money may be clear-cut for Gabrielle, but it is actually rather confusing when we try to address employees' needs. While employee surveys rarely rank money high on their list of needs (it's usually about fifth), the fact is salary is usually the biggest thing advertised in help wanted ads. It is also the benchmark used when employees compare their career progress and the first thing out of his mouth when describing his job.

Because of this ambivalent perception, it is in vogue for organizational psychologists to disregard money when studying employee retention. That would be a mistake. While money is rarely an employee's top incentive, it is the one thing no employee would ever work without. So how do we handle the effect of compensation on attracting and retaining talent?

Compensation is a classic example of Maslow's theory in action. Everyone has determined a minimum standard of living that they simply must have. Understand that this base level varies dramatically from person to person. Someone just out of college has a different understanding of the term "minimum standard" than a thirty-five-year-old doctor with three kids does. Money is the only motivation for the employee until this minimum standard is achieved. However, once that is met, compensation quickly falls as a need and as an incentive. Money is always a factor, mind you, but becomes less important as the employee pursues other aspects of his life.

So, if a person's minimum standard is $25,000, you cannot attract or hold on to him no matter what other incentives are offered when you don't meet that minimum requirement. Grand titles, a plush office, free massages, a Nobel Prize—none of these matter if the salary is $22,000.

However, once his salary reaches $25,000, many other factors begin to come into play. (According to the theory, the next concern will be safety needs, such as job security.) Once you meet the $25,000 threshold, the next thousand dollars would be better spent on other aspects of his life that can be found further up the hierarchical pyramid.

You don't have be the highest bidder in order to attract and retain a great employee, but you do have to meet his basic needs in order to have the right to further compete for his attention. In short, compensation is a pass/fail issue. Once you have passed, other issues become more important.

Despite this fact, business owners still perceive cash as the ultimate cure-all. When in a retention crisis, such as when a key employee turns in her notice, the only tool pulled out of the box is I'll-pay-you-a-lot-more-money. It's an ineffective tool because money is rarely the real reason for the resignation. (In fact, money only becomes a factor when the offer is greater than a 20 percent increase.)

So, here is the bottom line on the bottom line: As long as his most basic needs are met, money is not a significant issue *unless the employee is making less working for you than he could earn from the majority of your competitors.* Keep your compensation levels in the 75th percentile in your area and industry and cash will rarely cause attrition.

MONEY AS A RETENTION CURE-ALL

When faced with an ongoing turnover crisis, many entrepreneurs may try to cure the problem by making large, across-the-board pay increases. While effective for the short-term, this is more likely a formula for long-term devastation. The graph below (Figure 13.1), keyed to the comments below, shows why this approach may sink your business.

a. Suppose you are having a retention crisis. This has been an ongoing issue affecting your business greatly and you choose to take forceful action.
b. You institute an across-the-board pay increase for your entire workforce.
c. You will indeed see an immediate and dramatic decline in turnover. Your workers will be overwhelmed by the gesture, forget all other problems, and also find themselves priced out of the market.
d. However, after a deceptive lull in resignations, the workers realize that all the things that were making them dissatisfied are still present. Turnover begins to slowly creep up again.
e. Other companies in your industry or market must compete for workers, so they meet or exceed the new wage standards you have set. Turnover accelerates to the point that your attrition crisis is now much greater than it was to start with.

Figure 13.1
Why Cash Won't Cure Turnover

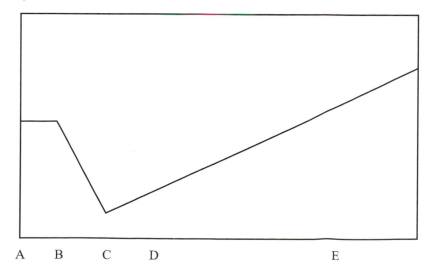

A   B   C   D   E

This graph is not an economic theory. It is solid reality. You will see a temporary drop in attrition if you use money as a solution. If the real needs are ignored, the turnover will undoubtedly climb to record levels.

ON THE OTHER HAND

You can cause your business irreparable harm if you use money as your solution for a general problem with high turnover. Of course, there is always an exception to everything. You could create a retention plan focusing completely on compensation. Especially in the sales field, compensation that is significantly higher than industry norms—let's say 25 percent higher—will attract a powerful, though mercenary, workforce. You do so at great peril. Your workers will be loyal to the cash, not the company. Also know that someday there will be someone who will be willing to pay them more. An ambitious, reckless upstart could take out your entire team in one bloody weekend. Also, if you choose this strategy, you must stick with it, regardless of economic cycles or fortunes of the company. A worker who is solely motivated by money will jump ship in a heartbeat if the money is ever reduced. I cannot think of a situation where I would recommend this strategy be used, but I wanted to address it before it crossed your mind. Of course, there is more to compensation than salary. Let's take a brief survey at some of the other features workers have come to expect in their total package.

BONUSES AND CONTESTS

The movie *Glengarry Glen Ross* explores the dark world of high-pressure sales. There is a powerful scene that shows how cutthroat the land sales business can be. The big boss rolls out a sales contest to motivate the staff. "Here are the prizes," he announces. "First place, a brand new Cadillac *El Dorado*. Second place, a set of steak knives. Third place, you're fired."

I've never seen a good bonus program. That includes about a dozen I have designed. In many fields, such as management and sales, people expect them as a part of the package, so let's put together a program that provides incentives not only for excellent performance but to also encourage retention. Here are some ideas:

- *Make the bonus an incentive for superior performance.* Too many bonus programs become entitlements. They are structured so that payment is made for not screwing up, rather than for achieving stellar results. Here are two ways you know it has become an entitlement program: (1) 95 percent of your employees achieve the goals, and (2) the other 5 percent grumble that they were counting on the money in order to make the rent payment. Instead of paying an entitlement, use some of the money to raise everybody's pay and then install a true performance-based bonus program.
- *Install a true performance-based bonus program.* Pick two or three important goals for your employees to achieve. Set high benchmarks for those goals. Pay huge chunks of cash for achieving those high benchmarks—so huge

that everyone will be straining with all their talents to hit the mark. Those who make this bonus will have delivered such great results that the money paid out is but a small fraction of the benefits delivered to the company.

- *Tie bonuses to tenure.* Pay your bonuses annually if you can, and offer the employee an option. He can get 100 percent of the money right now or he can delay the payment for a year and be paid 150 percent. However, as with many sweepstakes rules, you must be present to win. If the employee terminates within the year, he forfeits all payments. Also note that when the year has passed and he is about to collect the 150 percent payout, he has another decision to make.
- *Use non-cash payments.* Pay bonuses in stock options that mature in the future. The employee will get some gratification when the awards are made, but the real value does not appear until the employee has become a long-term team member.
- *Offer retention bonuses instead of sign-on bonuses.* Sign-on bonuses encourage employees to jump from job to job, while retention bonuses offer incentives for staying. Consider cash gifts or prizes (such as paid membership in a professional association or a health club membership) to mark anniversaries.

(*Note:* Bonus programs that apply to hourly—nonsalaried—workers can create payroll problems. To avoid unintended outcomes, check with a compensation specialist.)

KEEP IT SIMPLE AND EXCITING

While still in my twenties, I made the big plunge into the world of entrepreneurship. I purchased a historic dinner theater from the company I was then working for. Actually, I negotiated the deal with myself. Unfortunately, Ken the Seller was a much better negotiator than Ken the Buyer, and I immediately faced some wicked financial challenges.

I was energized and highly motivated when I held my initial staff meeting; I wanted people to have the same motivation as I began my first big venture. To help them understand how integral they were to the success of the business, I mentioned my intention to implement a profit-sharing plan.

I was asked about this incentive at a meeting several months later. "Yes," I replied, "We do have a profit-sharing plan." Their faces lit up until I added, "and each of you owe me eleven hundred dollars so far."

Your initial compensation plan should be competitive, motivating, and realistic. Don't package a bunch of features that may later prove to be weak programs. Keep it simple on the front end and add quality programs as your company grows.

BENEFITS

Thirty years ago, benefits were a minor add-on to the compensation "package." Other than health insurance (which was once rather inexpensive because nobody really knew how to cure many diseases), there really weren't many things added to the compensation beyond cash. However, creative minds went to work, expectations changed, and benefits grew from being a nice add-on to a significant chunk of payroll expenses. In fact, it is not unusual if the cost of the benefits exceed 50 percent of the employee's salary.

While there was a time in which benefits were considered extras and referred to as "perks," they are now an expected part of the package. Let's touch on some of the more popular benefits.

Absolutes

Let's start with the absolutes. You must offer these to even be allowed to compete for workers.

Health Insurance

The costs of healthcare has risen so dramatically over the past ten years that workers no longer expect you to pay all these costs of coverage. It is common for these costs to be shared by the employer paying for the employee and the employee paying for the family coverage. Another successful strategy is to offer a cafeteria plan and give the employee x dollars to apply against whatever features he wants. Use whatever formula for allocation that you can best afford, but the most important thing is to have a plan available. Most workers simply cannot accept any job in which health coverage is unavailable.

Vacation

An absolute if you want your employees to feel like they work for a real company.

Workers' Compensation

Yes, it is true that you are required by law to provide this to your employees. Just because you are required to do it doesn't mean it's not a benefit you provide. List this as a part of the many benefits you provide your employees. We'll discuss this in more detail later in this chapter.

Sick Leave

Most companies provide sick leave with specific plans that vary widely. On average, nine sick days are awarded each year. Many companies are now grouping sick days, holidays, and vacation days into a generic category called personal days. I like the concept of this grouping, but am leery of including sick days. Some employees, particularly the young invincible ones, may not accumulate their sick time and spend it on vacation. Thus, you are faced with a morale nightmare should the employee fall ill and have inadequate sick days available. Keep these separate, or at least require half of them to be accumulated only for illness.

Expected

Here are some benefits that, while not absolute requirements for the benefit package, certainly are expected by most workers today. You will not be able to compete for excellent talent if you leave many of these out.

Retirement Vehicle

Retirement plans are excellent retention tools on so many levels. Besides the fact that employees now demand ways to protect their future security, a retirement plan sets up the expectation that you plan for employees to stay with your company until they retire.

Holidays

The number of holidays celebrated varies considerably among employers and industry, as well as by region of the country. Christmas and Thanksgiving are certainly absolutes, but this list has rapidly expanded in the past decade. Because of this variance, we often see the selection of holidays become a decisive issue rather than a cause for relaxation. (I was once with a company in which employees were given their birthdays off but did not recognize the Martin Luther King holiday.)

Let me make a recommendation on how to deal with holidays so they are a great benefit but do not hurt your operations: Decide on the number of holidays you will celebrate each year. In this example, let's say ten days. Then, pick two or three that the business will celebrate as a whole and close for the day (perhaps, Thanksgiving, Christmas, and Independence Day). Convert the other seven days to *personal days*. The employee can do whatever he wants with those days—celebrate Columbus Day, enjoy his birthday, add them to a vacation, or simply have an occasional long weekend. Here is the added benefit for you: your company now has operational flexibility. Your offices or stores can stay open throughout the year, staffed by people who have no objection to working on holidays that hold little significance to them.

Other Insurance

Standard offerings include long- and short-term disability protection and dental coverage. These costs can often be passed to the employee, but it is more typical that the employer pays for a portion.

Bereavement Leave

Early in his career, my friend Jim was in an accident and broke several bones, which put him out of work for six weeks. The company had an excellent short-term disability policy and had no issue with his being at home recuperating for that long. Several years later, his sister unexpectedly died. He took the three days off, just as the company's bereavement policy allowed, and then returned to work. One day he passed by his boss's office and overheard him telling a co-worker, "I know it's tough to lose a sister, but it has been three weeks. Jim needs to get over it or start looking for another job."

MegaGlobal must be arbitrary in the enforcement of its benefits and policies. You can show some flexibility.

World Class

The first two categories, absolutes and expected, are defensive tactics and will help you *reduce turnover*. World class benefits are an offensive weapon and will *encourage retention*. Adding these benefits will generate strong employee loyalty. Your employees will point to these as examples of your being a great employer.

Still More Insurance

Basic benefits include health insurance, but look for opportunities to add other protection: additional life, disability, dental, and specialty policies can be arranged through companies specializing in supplemental insurance. They will customize packages for each employee, usually offering reduced rates for your unofficial group. The cost for these policies can be passed along to the worker; all you have to do is provide a payroll deduction.

Educational Assistance

You reap two obvious benefits when reimbursing workers for their ongoing education. In addition to the obvious increase in employee loyalty, you are training her for a whole lot less than you could develop her yourself. Can't afford to absorb the full cost? That's OK; you'll gain a similar increase in reputation just by making the gesture of paying for some of the expenses. Start by offering to pay for the books or supplies or a percentage of the tuition.

Credit Union Membership

Credit unions deliver a wallop of savings for their members—you can set up this opportunity for your employees and it will cost you nothing.

Merchant Discounts

Form a cooperative with other businesses to offer each other's employees the same discount they provide their own workers. Check with local amusement parks, carpet cleaners, landscapers, restaurants, and movie theaters.

Adoption Aid

There is nothing—and I mean nothing—you can do to create permanent, deep gratitude than to help an employee with some of the huge expenses involved in adopting a child. Just like educational assistance, you don't have to pick up the whole tab to secure this loyalty; consider granting a couple of extra weeks paid leave or making a donation to the child's education fund.

Civic Duty Supplements

Giving an employee time off to perform jury duty is certainly not a benefit. This is because jury duty pays so little—in some cases, as little as $5 per day. The average worker is indeed making a sacrifice when ordered to miss work and fulfill his civic responsibilities. In fact, the effects can be financially devastating for those living paycheck-to-paycheck. Show your support for your community by paying your team member her full wages during those days.

I also recommend you do this for other employee civic service. Although you are not required to do so—and maybe *because* you are not required to do so—you will endure deep loyalty from National Guard members you keep on your payroll during their annual two weeks of camp. (When word gets out among fellow guardsmen, you'll also see added sales as well as pick up a nice recruiting advantage.)

Help Me Help You Help Me

What is your reaction to these benefits that many employees are asking for?

- On-site ATM
- On-site child care
- Free lunch or subsidized on-campus cafeteria
- Personal concierge services
- Dry cleaning services

I can guess what your reaction is to these benefits. You are saying: "Geez! The next thing you know, they'll be expecting me to peel their grapes for them." Enough is enough, right?

Let me ask you to view this list from a different perspective. Instead of thinking of these as more silly demands from spoiled workers, think of how these services would affect you and your business. Providing some of these luxuries might make your workers more productive and your life a little easier.

For instance, an on-site ATM prevents some lunch breaks from being extended. The same applies with bringing in a free lunch on Fridays or even having an on-site cafeteria. Studies show that employees are back at their desks much quicker when they don't have to leave to have lunch. The same benefits accumulate by providing other services on-site, such as dry cleaning pick-up/delivery or travel services.

Think of how an on-site child-care cooperative would affect your company. How often do workers miss work or are late for work because of child-care issues? See if a cooperative can be arranged among the workers in your office and other businesses in your office building. Doing this will get you branded as a hero and improve attendance. (Also consider the recruiting advantage you will have.) Some, or most of you, aren't yet in a position to offer such benefits, but one day you might be, and sooner than you think, so keep them in mind.

Take the Credit

You will build solid worker loyalty if you provide your team with a good benefit package—maybe. Let me illustrate that qualification by refer-ring to the classic movie, *Dr. Strangelove.*

In order to prevent nuclear war, a well-intentioned government agency builds a doomsday machine. This is a massive explosive device that will destroy the entire world if anyone uses a nuclear device. The reason this would save the world is because no one would be foolish enough to risk his own destruction. (When this movie was made, it was an accepted fact. Sadly, this logic no longer exists among some groups.) Nuclear war would, therefore, be eliminated. What ruined the whole concept, unfortunately, was that they built the doomsday device in secret. Naturally, it's useless if no one knows it exists.

The same goes for all those expensive perks and benefits you offer. It is all a terrible waste if you don't take credit for them. You will just spend a lot of money and see no change in retention. You must shout your benevolence from the mountaintop. At least annually, meet with each employee and provide them with a detailed explanation of all their benefits. Then tell them what those benefits cost you. They will be amazed. (So will you.) Un-announced benefits are as useless as a secret doomsday machine. Let them know of your generosity and reap the retention rewards this brings with it.

Yes, You Can

I know what you are thinking right now: *OK Ken, that was darn interest-ing. I can see how offering all those benefits would make my employees happy and secure. Have you forgotten that I'm not Exxon? I'm a small business with eight employees. I can't get those benefits for my people, can I?*

Yes you can. You may be able to provide the employees of your enter-prise with benefits every bit as good as those offered at MegaGlobal through what is called a Professional Employer Organization, or PEO. PEOs are relatively new business structures designed to offer human resource services to smaller companies. You can enjoy these services with as few as three employees.

Here how this works: A PEO forms a co-employment relationship with your company. While you still maintain complete control over your employees' work status and activities, they legally become part of the PEO's company for payroll and tax purposes. Insofar as purchasing benefits, your employees are no longer a part of a nine-person company, they are now a part of an employee base that is 30,000 strong. While they still work for your company by all other definitions, when it comes to receiving benefits they are part of a mega-corporation. These are high-quality benefits at a reasonable cost. I encourage you to explore this option for providing your employees with the same perks that the big boys provide theirs.

TRAINING

We touched on this subject in Chapter 5, but it bears another look as a basic job need. Employees need and deserve basic job training. I am not referring to career development; we'll deal with that in Chapter 14. Instead, we must first deal with giving workers quality instruction for performing their jobs competently and correctly.

Too many workers are tossed into positions immediately after being hired. This can be understood; critical work has been left undone while waiting for the position to be filled and the owner is eager to get things back to normal. The new employee appeared to be qualified and quite intelligent during the interview process, so let's have him jump right in.

I saw this episode repeated many times during my restaurant career; indeed, I must confess to often making this mistake myself. Regardless of the employee's high qualifications and the manager's good intentions, such a scene is destined for failure. An untrained worker lacks confidence and makes mistakes. He feels insecure in his skills and insecure about his ability to keep his job. Early turnover is usually the result of our failure to prepare our people. Always provide basic training to the employee from the very beginning. Do not lay any responsibility on a worker for which he is not properly trained or equipped.

PROVIDE A SAFE PLACE TO WORK

A safe workplace is an employee's basic right. Yes, safety does include those things monitored by OSHA, but that is not the focus of this section. Let's discuss the recent phenomenon of workplace violence: The workplace reflects society and, sadly, our society has become more accepting of violence as a problem-solving tool. While you cannot guarantee the complete abolition of violence in your workplace, there are some steps you can take to make it less likely.

- Do not tolerate joking about violence. Your policy should follow airport policies: all comments are taken seriously. "I was only joking," is not an accepted defense in sexual harassment suits and should not be accepted as an explanation for making violent threats.

- There is no such thing as "a small act of violence." Horseplay quickly evolves from innocent fun into a serious offense. Don't allow any type of abusive touching, no matter how slight it initially appears to be.
- Ban threatening words or behavior. These often precede violent acts. Cut it off at the earliest opportunity.
- Ban all weapons. Despite the attempts of my own state legislature (Georgia) and others to prevent you from doing this, forbid weapons anywhere on your property. This includes employees who have guns in their cars in your parking lot. (An angry or mentally disturbed employee is not inconvenienced by having to walk to the parking lot to retrieve his shotgun.)
- Do thorough background checks.
- Strictly enforce existing security procedures. Do not allow employees to ignore procedures that you put in place for their safety. Allowing unauthorized visitors, propping doors open, and leaving entrances unlocked are all actions that have gotten people killed.

You must create a safe workplace. Employees will stay in an environment of fear only until they can find a safer place to work.

HARASSMENT-FREE ZONE

Harassment will negate all your efforts to build a solid, enthusiastic team. It will kill productivity, morale, and all sense of community. You know this. In fact, this is so engrained in your management philosophy that you probably think there is no need for this section. Please stick with me, though, because there is a form of harassment you have probably not considered: the office bully.

The bully is often overlooked, perhaps because of the almost playful label he is given. The label *bully* kind of reminds us of junior high school, doesn't it? Despite the terminology, know that the bully is a bigger cause of turnover than any other form of harassment. The office gossip is a bully; so is the person who makes undercutting remarks about another employee's work or personal habits.

Bullying behavior often begins innocently, often as a just-a-bit-over-the-line joke that is quickly followed by "just kidding." However, it soon develops into a organized blast of verbal assaults and cutting remarks. Threats can often emerge as the bully gorges himself on this compensating power trip.

I am not overstating this problem. A University of North Carolina survey of 775 people who said they had been treated rudely or disrespectfully at work showed the devastating impact. Most of those surveyed reported missing significant amount of work time as they worried about the bully or tried to avoid him; 12 percent actually quit their jobs rather than dealing with the bully any longer.

I'll won't explore all the psychological analyses of the bully and or dwell further on the impact on the victim. I will just make two points: (1) Bullying is devastating to your team, and (2) It is your responsibility to stop it.

Always recognize that you must accept responsibility for solving the problem. Never deal with such issues by having employees "work it out among themselves." They can't. It would not be an issue if they were able to work it out among themselves. This approach is just using a tired cliché to avoid your responsibilities. Take charge.

One last (passionate) point: Sometimes management shies away from firing the bully because he is an outstanding performer. I have only one thing to say to a manager who slinks from responsibility because of the fear of lost revenue: *Shame on you*.

Yes, it is hard to lose a superstar sales executive, but it must happen. Being an employer is a sacred trust. Your first responsibility is to the people who have merged their livelihoods with your dreams. You have no greater duty than to prevent their dignity from being threatened by a power-seeking, compensating bully, regardless of the bags of silver he generates. If you shirk that core responsibility, then you have forfeited any claim to the respect and loyalty of your employees.

JOB SECURITY

My mouth dropped when I read that a major electronics retailer had announced their strategy for controlling costs. They were going to lay off all the salespeople making above-average commissions and replace them with cheaper hires. This strategy is preposterous on so very many levels, but let's just focus on one for the moment. By executing this strategy, the company has permanently destroyed a basic need of all employees, the need for job security. These employees will spend the rest of their (probably brief) tenure looking over their shoulders, fearful that any mistake will cost them their job. (Actually, in this case, the employees will actually be afraid to *excel*!)

Is job security a basic need? You cannot fully realize the need human beings have for security until you consider the fact that kamikaze pilots wore crash helmets. Despite the shift from a philosophy of lifetime employment to a free-agency style career system, the need for job security is still critical to the average employee. Yes, the worker is now more willing to change jobs several times during his career, but he wants to be the one who initiates those changes. The threat of a layoff—in fact, just a tiny rumor to that affect—is enough to preoccupy his mind to the point of dysfunction. There is nothing that will kill an employee's spirit quicker than losing his livelihood because of something beyond his control.

Please understand that I am not suggesting that you cannot do what you have to do to save your business. Sometimes economic reality requires a reduction in force just to keep the company afloat. However, layoffs must be reserved for survival. Using layoffs as a knee-jerk solution to small, temporary issues is ignorant. Using layoffs or reorganizations to manipulate stock prices is unconscionable.

If a company dangles employment security over their heads, the company can forfeit the trust and respect of its workers forever. This is where you have a dramatic advantage over your big competitors. Despite the initial perception, small businesses such as yours offer much greater job security than the global competitors. How's that? The big guys often create and dispose of positions with little thought or planning. A product is brought to market and a large workforce is added. The product fails and the department is wiped out. You can place much greater attention in each person you hire and each position created.

MegaGlobal has a rather arbitrary discipline process (1-2-3 and you are out) and a general people-treatment template designed to avoid lawsuits and discrimination claims. You, on the other hand, can treat your employees individually, understand their issues, and work closely with them to correct any performance difficulties. Your employees are less likely to face unfair or arbitrary termination than those working for the big established companies.

Layoffs are a common tool of management to manipulate stock processes. That is not a tool you whip out, because you are interested in growth and profits more than image and stock prices. Let's face it. A small workforce often becomes family. While in the end you must do what is best for your business and its survival, the fact is you will try just about every other solution before you will eliminate people you have come to care about personally.

My point? Almost by definition, you provide your workers greater job security than the giant corporations provide their workers. This does not mean that you must guarantee lifetime employment to your workers, nor does it mean that you shirk from hard choices. It most certainly does not mean that poor performers, troublemakers, or thieves should be kept on the payroll. What it does mean is that you operate with the *intent* of providing secure employment for those people who have joined your team. As an entrepreneur, you don't have a lot of control over many things, but you do have complete control over your intent. Operate with the intent to provide job security to your team members and watch how deep their loyalties will grow.

We've reviewed some of the needs you must address in order to keep your team. Again realize that these are just the basics, the absolute minimum required for you to consider yourself an employer. By being an entrepreneur, there is no way you will ever settle for doing the absolute minimum on anything. If you choose to excel, you must now look to address the more advanced needs of your team. Let's move from meeting your employees' *job* needs into a more fulfilling area: meeting their *career* needs.

14

Filling Career Needs

Chapter 13 discussed your employees' most basic needs. These needs are your "cost of entry" to a specific pool of labor and merely give you the right to compete. Many people do hold jobs and are indeed satisfied just to have their most basic needs met. These are usually temporary or part-time jobs and, while the worker may find the job acceptable, it is viewed as "just a job" nonetheless.

You would not be reading this book if all you wanted to do is provide "just a job" to your workers. You want to develop a team and offer challenging, rewarding, and enriching careers. That's what we address in this chapter. Let's look at how you can retain your fine team members by addressing their *career* needs.

THE NEED FOR COMMUNITY

Once upon a time in America, there was a clear understanding of what the word community meant. Perhaps, we each defined that from the TV shows we watched. Beaver Cleaver's neighborhood, Opie's Mayberry, even Bart Simpson's Springfield have all imprinted an image of a community as a place composed of our neighborhoods, our schools, and our houses of worship.

This has not been completely replaced in our society, but we have added a new institution to that list. Today, the workplace is part of that community. Today, we look to our jobs to fulfill needs that we once sought from neighbors. You play a significant role in your workers' need for relationships.

THE RELATIONSHIP WITH THE BOSS

Most workers spend more time with their bosses than with their spouses. Is there any wonder why the employee's relationship with the boss is often the most significant source of both pleasure and pain in his life. Perhaps that is why (as we learned earlier) the manager is the most significant influence in retaining employees.

Unfortunately, it is beyond the scope of this book to fully examine how to become a good manager. It just cannot be done within the limits of a small section in a single chapter. Rather than attempting this, we'll underscore the need for healthy employee/management relationships and look at some ways to make that happen.

Your primary task is to simply employ good managers. Hire supervisors with excellent people skills and primarily evaluate their job performance based on those skills. While this may seem obvious, most managers get their jobs through demonstrations of technical skills rather than relationship abilities. This is why so many people promoted internally fail at the new management job. She may be the best mechanic in the garage but never had any experience leading people. Only when she has crashed and burned is it realized that the only qualification she had to be a manager is excellent product knowledge. Choose managers based on their ability to manage.

By the way, this also applies to annual performance reviews. Too often, this review focuses on the technical aspects of the job and only devotes token acknowledgement to the manager's people skills and human resources accomplishments. You can expect what you inspect: pay slim attention to the manager's people skills and you can be assured those abilities will atrophy. Identify the poor managers in your business. Here are a few ways to identify people who don't relate well with their workers:

- A bad manager will constantly talk about all the lousy employees you have assigned her. Even if she did the hiring herself, she'll complain about their unacceptable performance.
- A poor manager does not take equity in his team. Rather than working with his people and improving their performance, he will expect someone else (you) to give him new "off-the-rack" workers who are immediately perfect.
- If your business is large enough to have several similar workgroups, you will see lots of transfer requests to get out of her department.
- You will receive many complaints from his employees, not necessarily directed at the manager. It's just that they have gotten so used to being unhappy that the employees become angry in general.
- Poor managers do not develop their people. Look for a department where performance declines or promotions rarely occur and you will find it headed by a manager with poor people skills.
- Here's some circular logic for you: you can easily identify lousy managers by looking at their turnover rates.

Once you have identified the poor managers, you must work with them to develop their people skills and hold them accountable for instilling high employee morale. They must be removed if they cannot change. (What about how the manager's turnover will affect your retention rate? Losing her will save you dozens of people in the future. It is a net gain for the retention stats.)

THE RELATIONSHIP WITH CO-WORKERS

Much of what I said about the manager also applies to other employees. It is indeed a morale-killer to dislike your boss, but at least you can get away from him occasionally. How about the worker in the adjoining cubicle? How about the partner assigned with you in a patrol car, production line, or maintenance truck? You are stuck with them and their attitude for the full eight hours. Resentments accumulated during those eight hours will soon be transferred to your customers. Even as a defensive sales strategy, you must ensure positive relationships between your workers. How do we deal with people with poor people skills? Here are some ideas:

- Hold people accountable. Pull the employee aside and directly let her know it is an issue that must be solved. Let her know you will work with her, help to find solutions, but you expect her to correct the problem.
- Let people know your expectations. Make it clear that you feel their ability to work and play well with others is just as important as their technical skills.
- Don't ignore squabbling employees. If they tend to get along with others but seem to only direct their animosity toward each other, physical separation might help. Don't end it there. Band-Aid solutions rarely last; employees must work together to find a truce.
- And if the employee cannot change her attitude, the solution is the same as with a manager. You cannot let one person infect the atmosphere of the workplace. Perhaps you can get her a job with one of your competitors.

Here's a trick I once used to deal with two feuding workers. I sent them to clean a window, assigning one on the outside and the other on the inside. They were soon laughing and making goofy faces at one another while they scrubbed, and stayed buddies for the rest of the day.

Now that was all rather negative, wasn't it? Sorry about the approach, but my theory is that *good* relationships are actually the social norm. Positive relationships more often come from an absence of negatives rather than an accumulation of positives. (People are liked until they give a reason to be hated.)

Let's look at some ways you can create a sense of community in your business.

Celebrate Everything

Look for ways to have light-hearted moments in your office. Certainly celebrate birthdays and employment anniversaries, but also look to mark important days in the company's life. Celebrate the day you opened your first store, the day you incorporated, the anniversary of a new product line, or the last audit of the tax season. Use these events to create your own company holidays.

Sponsor Outside Activities

Your employees will work better as a team inside the office if they behave like teams outside the office. You see this with the plethora of company-sponsored softball teams, bowling leagues, and even book clubs. Many companies will pay for health club memberships, knowing that the employees may go as a group after they get off work in the evenings.

Develop Family-Friendly Programs

If you want her family to support the company, then you should do things that support the family. You can do this through adopting flexible work schedules so your employees can have more family time. Give prizes to the kids for great report cards. Let spouses play on any sports teams and participate in every company-sponsored social activity. Encourage family members to visit the office and have lunch with the employee and his co-workers.

Here is my favorite example of a company including the family: FedEx conducts a lottery whenever it adds a new plane to its fleet and the winner sees the plane named after his or her child. Perhaps you don't have any unchristened airplanes in the parking lot, but you can include the child in the background of one of your print ads. Betcha you can come up with a few ideas that fit your business.

Encourage Employee Friendships

Working together outside of the office will help them work better from nine to five. By addressing this important human need, you will not only make life easier in the office. Studies have shown that retention is far higher in organizations when their employees have strong personal connections and feel a sense of community.

THE NEED FOR PERSONAL FULFILLMENT

Why would a man risk his life for a colorful ribbon? Why would a doctor turn her back on a $300,000 salary and volunteer to work in a small African clinic? Why would a pilot continue to fly jet fighters for $60,000 a year when he could earn four times that amount flying a commercial 747? If you had no problem understanding their motivations, then you have probably climbed to the top of Maslow's pyramid. Most entrepreneurs are indeed at that life summit—developing their own business ventures is an expression of their need to self-actualize.

Many of your employees will also be at this point in their lives. Indeed, most of the people you will want to attract are usually at the stage where they crave recognition and assistance in reaching their dreams. For a concerned and caring employer, addressing an employee's need for personal fulfillment can address your same need.

Personal fulfillment is a category I use to combine the two highest levels of human need: self-esteem and what Maslow referred to as self-actualization. We address self-esteem by showing the employee he is valued and by loudly recognizing his efforts. We also help the team member self-actualize by providing challenging job assignments, career training, and assisting him in discovering opportunities to help his co-workers and community. Let's begin this rewarding journey by looking at ways we can help our team members feel valued.

PERSONAL VALUE

I've never had a bad boss. I've learned from every person I have been exposed to in my career. Perhaps the best motivator I have known is Clint Clark. At the time I knew him, he was the CEO of a company in which I served as a regional vice president. One day, I made an unexpected visit to the corporate office. I bumped into Clint as I stepped into an elevator. Clint smiled broadly and gave me a lapel pin that said, "Customer service is #1." There is no one in this company who cares more about our customers than you, Ken. I want to present this to you personally."

Wow. I was stunned. No one had ever paid me such a rich compliment, much less the president of a major corporation. However, it probably would have meant even more if he hadn't been holding a box containing ten thousand of those pins. Even though he was snowing me a bit, the fact remained that Clint was taking the time to snow me. It remained a magical moment in my career.

I had the opportunity to pass along some of this motivation a few weeks later. I was visiting a restaurant I had not seen for many months and was astounded with the wonderful improvements made in its operation. I called the manager over, removed that pin from my jacket, and said to him, "Here. Clint Clark gave this to me, but I am so proud of what you have done here that I want you to have it." He was close to tears as I placed it on his shirt.

I made a strong impact on that manager by demonstrating my appreciation the same way it was shown for me (although I did kick it up a notch by having only one pin with me). The story doesn't end there. I had been gone from that company for several years when one day I had the occasion to visit that same store for lunch. The same manager was still there, and he was still wearing that lapel pin.

It is amazing how simple acts of appreciation can yield such dynamic results. In fact, the simplest and least expensive gesture delivers the biggest impact of all motivation tools, yet few managers use it effectively. In fact, Wichita State University studied 1,500 employees on the subject of motivation in the workplace. The study concluded that the most powerful motivator was to simply thank the worker for a job well done. Yet, even though this gesture cost nothing, only 42 percent of these workers had ever been recognized in this manner.

Ponder this: It costs little or nothing to tell an employee that she is appreciated. Doing so has a dramatic effect on retention. Yet, it is a rarely used tool. Why is this? We'll give the empty managers the benefit of the doubt and assume they just can't think of novel ways to do this. So let me start a list of inexpensive ways you can recognize an employee for her good efforts. Use the margins of this book to list your own ideas.

- Have the team member come into your office and just say thanks. Discuss no other issues during the very brief visit.
- Take the employee and spouse to lunch.
- Give him the afternoon off. Throw in a couple of tickets for a ball game or movie.
- Local newspapers, especially online blogs, are hungry for news content. Send them a press release bragging about your employee.
- Send her an e-mail expressing appreciation for her excellent work. Also, copy the entire company.
- Write a letter to his family explaining how important he is to your firm.
- Publicize achievements in the company newsletter. (I like to have a column called "Caught in the Act.")
- Prepare a complete breakfast for your team to mark an accomplishment or for putting in extra hours on a project.

Never overlook the simplest, most meaningful tool for showing appreciation: be liberal in your distribution of thank you actions and gestures. There is nothing that has a greater impact than looking a team member in the eye and saying, "Thank you!"

SCHEDULE SPONTANEITY

The trouble with being spontaneous is that it just doesn't happen on a regularly scheduled basis. It's too easy to forget to make gestures to workers. Time passes and despite your best intentions, you stop showing regular gestures of appreciation. (With the possible exception of an occasionally grunted "thanks.")

Here's what we'll do about that. Right now—yep, I mean right now—pull out your daily planner. Write one employee's name above each week. During that employee's week, watch for her to do something right. When you catch her doing it, immediately explain what you saw, tell her why it is important, and lavish praise for his achievement. Don't wait for her to accomplish something earth shattering; celebrate the most routine of acts. Don't worry that you won't catch her doing something noteworthy. I assure you that if you watch, you will find many praiseworthy acts.

PROMOTE PEER RECOGNITION

No recognition is as sweet as that coming from your neighbor. An employee feels great pleasure when her boss recognizes a good performance, but there is another level of satisfaction when she is cited by her peers as being worthy of their admiration.

Here is a good example: Watch the comments made by players selected to play in baseball's all-star game. Sure, those who win the fans' ballots get a kick out of winning the popularity contest, but the proudest all-stars are those reserves chosen by the other players. Nothing exceeds the satisfaction of being recognized by the people who know you best.

- A telecom company in Jacksonville, Florida, provides all employees with a notepad featuring the words "thank you" written in the background. Employees use these notes to send messages of appreciation to their peers whenever they notice a "noteworthy" action. Workers plaster the walls of their cubicles with these notes and consider a cluttered wall a badge of honor.
- A flooring manufacturer published a book called *The Master Salesman* containing the wisdom of its top salespeople. You can imagine the prestige felt by these executives seeing their peers learn from their experiences.
- Many companies declare an *Employee of the Month*. Let me make this suggestion: The award will carry much more clout if the employees make this selection rather than management. Harvey recounts this experience:

> One day I was particularly pleased with a project one of my employees had completed. To emphasize how much I appreciated his work, I sent an e-mail to all the employees (all six of them) naming him *Employee of the Month*. Initially this created some good-natured ribbing but the idea eventually caught on. Every so often, an employee will nominate a peer as employee of the month in recognition for an achievement or kind act the peer had noticed. All they get is an e-mail they can hang in their office, but they do appreciate it.

The Magic of Titles

An employer tried a little experiment when recruiting his sales team. He offered each member of the new team a choice of titles; they could be either a salesperson or a sales manager. Despite a little extra pay for salespersons, most chose to be sales managers.

Titles do carry prestige and this supports a human's need for recognition. You don't have to get silly, deceptive, or even manipulative with this—just look for opportunities to express job titles in more prestigious terms. Your administrative assistant could become Senior Administrator, a plumber can be a Master Plumber, and the bookkeeper becomes the Head Bookkeeper. Don't expect your employees to immediately acknowledge this change. In fact, many of them might even snicker when you tell them their new title. Keep looking; it won't be long before you'll see them change their nameplate, order new business cards, and prominently include the new title beneath their signature.

HELP THEM GROW

Harvard Business Review declared that the number one reason GenXers quit a job is because of lack of training. This generation puts strong emphasis on learning and the continual development of their skills. You must commit to their development if you want to keep them on your payroll. This also applies to the recruitment of GenXers; they will not make a commitment to you until you have committed to their development.

This, of course, applies to all your team members to a varying extent. While not all of your employees will seek to be developed into a CEO, most people do want to do their job better and learn new skills. Look at some of these avenues for expanding your team members' horizons:

Give Everyone a Mentor

Use some of your more experienced workers to coach the newer ones. This will not only benefit the "mentee," but also expand the senior worker's own sense of self-actualization.

Have Employees Conduct Seminars

If you look deeply, you will find a real gold mine in your cubicles. Your team members bring more skills with them than just those they use directly on the job. Chances are someone has experience in a business discipline you haven't used yet, such as a software program. Another member of your team may have construction or architectural skills he used in a previous career. I know of one company that was lucky enough to employ a former 911 operator who held weekly classes in CPR and other emergency procedures.

Keep the Lights On

Discuss company problems with your entire team, not just those directly involved in their solution. Explain your reasons for making your decisions so that your employees will learn how to approach business issues. (An added benefit is that someone might have a better idea.) Use your company as a living case study; those who want to learn will absorb tremendous, career-enhancing information. Make them more valuable employees.

Use Performance Reviews to Plan Development

Most performance reviews spend too much time playing *gotcha* with the past and no time learning how to do better in the future. Shift your focus during the annual review; work with the employee to design a practical and personal development plan.

Make sure the plan actually helps the person grow rather than just addressing deficiencies. There is a temptation to simply select the employee's weakest skill for development. Doing so will probably be ineffective. First of all, if it is the employee's weakest area, he probably isn't interested in the subject and he certainly will not be enthusiastic about completing programs in that area. An unenthused student will not learn. Instead, select one of his strengths. The chances are he will be eager to spend more time on a subject in which he shows great skill. You will get much better results by exploiting his strengths rather than chipping away at his weaknesses. (This is assuming that he meets minimum standards in all job-critical areas.)

Here is an example: I am a lousy golfer. On a good day, I will shoot in the high 200s. If you don't let me cheat, the score will approach 325. Seriously. I could take lessons, but even Tiger Woods would not be able to get my score below 175. True, that would be remarkable improvement, but I would still be the laughingstock of the clubhouse. A lot of time, money, and misery would have been absolutely wasted. However, you could invest that same time, money, and effort into one of my strengths, and I just might be able to move mountains. When developing your employees, develop their strengths.

Redeploy

Many jobs, particularly manufacturing or administrative ones, can become boring. These workers are susceptible to turnover, leaving your routine job for another company's boring routine. Besides looking for ways to make jobs more interesting, consider internal job-hopping. Cross train workers in dull jobs and allow them to rotate positions.

AT&T has a program called *Resource Link*. This is essentially an in-house temp agency. Departments post their needs, workers post their skills, and matches are made. Please note that this approach is not only for hourly workers. Engineers and managers can also be stuck in ruts and eagerly seek cross-departmental assignments.

Don't write this off just because you are a small company. You can fight job boredom by letting employees get involved in other tasks while still doing their assigned job. A billing clerk would enthusiastically serve an internal team that is considering a new advertising campaign. Your receptionist may enjoy helping the bookkeepers during month-end closing activities. That fellow in the corner with his head buried in the computer monitor—betcha he would love writing the monthly newsletter. Look for opportunities to enhance jobs through cross-functional assignments.

Invest in your team by developing their skills and knowledge. They will be stronger, happier, more productive, and less inclined to leave your company. Are you afraid you'll lose them if they broaden their capabilities? You might. But here is a scarier thought: *what if you don't develop them and they stay?*

THE HIGHEST LEVEL OF EMPLOYEE COMMITMENT

Martha Taft proudly introduced herself to her second grade classmates. ''My great grandfather was president of the United States,'' she began. ''My grandfather was a senator and my father is ambassador to Ireland. And I," she added with the most enthusiasm, "am a Brownie!"

We reach the point of self-actualization at various times in our lives. In fact, as our lives cycle, we may have this great need *several* times during our lives. While some folks satisfy their most lofty need through personal or family activities, many now use their career as the route to this summit. You will receive the deepest possible loyalty from an employee if you actively partner with him to fulfill this most mature need.

Some professions offer easier opportunities for this partnership than others. Researchers at drug companies can easily see how they are working to cure disease. A stonemason can feel a part of eternity by building a great cathedral. Firefighters know that there is no greater calling than to protect the lives of their neighbors.

Your company does not have to have a world-changing goal and your employees do not have to hold lofty positions in order to meet their needs for self-actualization. There are many projects and tasks that will address their needs. We discussed some of these earlier, such as holding seminars, mentoring young employees, and teaching CPR to your team (and their families). Keep your eyes open and you will often overhear a team member mention a situation or activity that he "would really like to do." You don't have to be awarded a Nobel Peace Prize in order to attain self-actualization (though, I admit, I would kill for one of those); there are many projects that will allow a person to feel her skills are making a contribution.

Perhaps you have drawn a blank as you ponder ways to help your workers attain their self-actualization needs. Until in-house opportunities become available, help the team members make a contribution outside your four walls. Sponsor your assistant as the company representative in a charity walk-a-thon. Let a team work building houses with Habitat for Humanity. Pay for a clerk to get his college degree in art history. Give an employee time off—or even a leave of absence—to make a mission trip with her church.

You can create a sense of mission and purpose with your employees. Doing so will not only make them more satisfied with their lives, it will firmly ingrain loyalty towards you and your company. Besides, helping an employee attain this satisfaction will also enhance your personal self-actualization.

> Alfred had just celebrated his fiftieth birthday—a point at which many men look back and take stock of their lives. Alfred was no exception and he took a long walk in the forest to contemplate his future.
>
> He was about a mile into his trek when a frog hopped onto his path. The varmint stopped suddenly and sat right at Alfred's feet. Then something quite odd happened. The frog spoke.
>
> "Please sir, hear me out," she began in a lovely voice. "I am not really a frog. I am actually a beautiful young princess. An evil witch cast this spell on me. But if you will kiss me, the spell will be broken and once

again I will become a beautiful princess. And if you will do that, I will serve you the rest of your life."

"Well I'll be darned," Alfred said. He reached down, carefully picked up the creature, and placed her gently into his pocket.

"What are you doing!" the princess frog cried. "I said that if you kiss me I will become a beautiful princess! I'll serve you in any way you desire! Didn't you hear me?"

"Yeah, I heard you," Alfred said as he continued his walk. "But at this point in my life, I think I would rather have a talking frog."

Unless you have only one employee, everyone on your entire team will have different needs. Since each of those team members will have different needs at different times in his life, you must continually rediscover your employees' needs.

Filling employees' needs is not similar to hitting a target. It is not even similar to hitting several different targets. In order to have a great retention rate, you must hit several different moving targets! Meeting the needs of your team members is a tough assignment. If you accomplish this, you will have a greater chance of keeping all those amazing people you worked so hard to recruit and develop. It's worth the hard work.

15

Holding On and Fighting Back

Our church asks us to fill out an attendance sheet each week so they can keep up with each of its 7,500 members. Usually, you just sign your name so they will know you are still around, but if there is a change in your status—such as address or phone number—you are supposed to make a note of the changes so the church can adjust its records.

Thus began my first great crisis when I reached my fiftieth birthday. It didn't really bother me to admit my milestone. What bothered me was the way I was supposed to report it. Ages were grouped; for instance, 13–19 or 25–35, and I was expected to check the little box beside the group marked *50 and over*. As I made that change on my data sheet, I realized that I would never again move to another category. This was it. I will be considered "50 and over" until I died. Right then, I began my long-delayed mid-life crisis.

Things happen to us that often prompt a reexamination of our lives. Sometimes our reaction to life's events is positive, such as losing weight or going back to school. Other reactions are neutral, possibly silly, like buying that proverbial shiny sports car. Unfortunately, some reactions become destructive, such as divorce. Many people direct their frustration towards their jobs.

Good managers watch for these life changes and know the potential impact on their employees' careers. This chapter will show you how to spot these trends to help you catch potential turnover early (while you can still successfully address it). In fact, let's explore a whole realm of defensive strategies and learn how we can best save our at-risk employees.

RECOGNIZING POTENTIAL TURNOVER

Hurricanes, volcanoes, and rattlesnakes all give some warning before they explode. So do employees. If a letter of resignation surprises you, then you just haven't been paying attention. There are several methods you can use to identify employees who are on the fast track towards attrition.

Open Your Eyes and Just Look Around

You know your team members well enough to sense when someone is behaving differently. For instance, one of the first indications of an unhappy employee is a change in their attitude. Is a former "cheerleader" now griping about minor issues? Perhaps an employee who had been an eager problem solver develops an apathetic attitude. Take note whenever a usually positive worker shifts into becoming a negative influence. Also look closely at employees showing a drop in productivity. The worker who normally has no problems exceeding his quota now delivers only minimum acceptable work. Someone who usually participates at meetings suddenly withdraws and stops offering suggestions. The team member who was known for working late each day is now a dedicated clock watcher. Look for people who are now taking an unusual number of sick days or who seem to be leaving work early quite often. They may be burned out or they could be spending that time traveling to job interviews. (Also take note when a worker seems to be dressed better on the days he is taking the afternoon off. He's either going to court, a funeral, or an interview.)

American pop culture has provided us with a sure-fire sign that an employee is unhappy: She will show her cynical side by posting *Dilbert* cartoons in her office. Employees doing this are sending a message, subconsciously begging you to ask her what's on her mind.

Watch for Life Changes

Because the workplace is the new community, people often express all life issues by taking it out on their jobs. I've seen an indication of this so often while looking at job applications. When explaining why they left previous jobs, applicants will often list "got divorced" or "mother died" as their reason. Though everyone reacts differently to personal crises, it would be wise for you to pay special attention when team members have a special event in their lives. It is time to take their temperature when:

- His last child leaves the nest or graduates from college.
- He receives an MBA or other advanced degree.
- There is a divorce or death in the family.
- He has a birthday that ends in a zero.

Certainly watch for potential turnover when work-related crises occur. Put the employee on suicide watch whenever a work decision may impact team members. Here are some examples:

- A boss or mentor retires or moves to a different company.
- A friend turns in his notice.
- She doesn't get a promotion that she wanted.
- An anticipated raise or bonus doesn't materialize as hoped.
- He wins a major award from a trade association.

SAVE THOSE WHO CAN BE SAVED

There are a number of people in this category.

Save the Poor Performer

"I need your permission to fire him, Bill." It was my first multi-unit supervisory job and I wanted to get rid of a manager who was particularly difficult to motivate. The company required that my boss sign off on any terminations.

"Are you sure you can't save him?" Bill asked.

"I'm sure," I stated with confidence. "Chuck has a lousy attitude and you just can't turn around a bad attitude."

Bill replied firmly, "Ken, the reason you can't turn around a bad attitude is because you've never tried."

Bill was right and taught me a lesson that day that I eventually based a career on. Too many people are terminated that could be saved. Some are slower learners who were close to competence just before the button was pushed. Others were lacking an easily taught skill. Still others were destined for the dustpan, but we'll just never know.

Let's look at some ways we can retain some of those workers who could, with the right approach, go from being another turnover statistic to being productive team members.

Talk to Him

Many employees are shocked when they are terminated; they honestly didn't know their performance was substandard. Always have an honest, thorough conversation with the employee before lowering the ax. Lay out the details of your expectations and tell her exactly where she falls short. This often does the trick all by itself.

Review Job Match

Remember that this is the biggest cause of turnover, so this is where you should look first. If she is not suited to the job, consider a transfer or modification of the job description.

Evaluate the True Issues

Be sure you have isolated the right problems. Because of the halo effect, we often feel that if an employee is doing one thing wrong, he must be doing everything wrong. Evaluate the worker's complete performance. Make note of the good as well as bad. Doing so will help you put all the issues in perspective as well as isolate the exact areas for improvement. (You would be surprised how many performance improvement plans consist of nothing more than "*You need to do better.*")

Put It into Perspective

How significant is the deficient skill or performance within the scope of the entire job? Don't allow a receptionist's lousy typing skills (which she rarely needs to use) overshadow her incredible abilities to welcome your clients. It's OK for an otherwise amazing employee to be substandard in rarely used skills as long as everyone is aware of the issue and accommodations are made to handle the tasks in a different manner.

Provide All Necessary Training

Never make a partial effort. Yes, this may be expensive but is really just peanuts when you amortize it over the long career of the now-productive employee.

Have Someone Else Try

You are not always going to be able to save every employee, but someone else may be able to save this one. Don't give up on anyone until you've let someone else work with him. It doesn't necessarily have to be an authority figure; many people respond better to peers. Select a mentor who not only understands the job but has exceptional mentoring skills.

When All Else Fails

Mark Twain's advice for improving a worker's performance was: "If at first you don't succeed, try, try, again. And then give up. No sense being a damn fool about it." Seriously, there does come a point when you (and probably the employee, too) recognize that things are just not going to work out. The employee must move on. Help him find another position and then wish him well. Be at peace knowing you have made every reasonable effort to hold on to your team members.

Don't Do This

I've avoided using the phrase "make every effort" because there are some things you shouldn't do when dealing with an employee having performance issues. First of all, don't consider suspensions. While suspensions may be a good tool for *conduct* issues, using them for performance problems will only guarantee resentment. Don't punish poor performance, improve it.

On the other hand, don't reward it either. Well-intentioned managers often make the mistake of dangling a carrot, such as a bonus, in front of substandard performers. Bonuses should be reserved for exceptional performance. Using them for the opposite will do nothing but create resentment in the workforce. Above all else, don't ignore the problem hoping it will eventually take care of itself. It won't. You must act.

Save the Retiree

We thoroughly examined the arena of recruiting retired workers in Chapter 2, so I won't replow that ground. However, this is a good time to consider the subject from a different angle: retaining any workers you have retiring from your company. Most people do not like the leap from forty-plus-hour workweeks to zero-hour workweeks. A transition period from full-time to part-time could provide you with several years of contributions from these deeply skilled employees. Consider hiring them as consultants. Use them as mentors or trainers. Look for opportunities to use all the skills, knowledge, and client contacts these people still possess.

Save the Employee Who Resigns

This is the most useless section in the book. When an employee hands you his letter of resignation, the chances of saving him are just short of zero. Why are your chances of success so slim? Here are a few to mull over:

- Others will perceive the concessions you make as unfair. This is because the concessions you make probably are unfair to others. You can screw up your entire team's dynamic by making knee-jerk changes to the way you treat just one person.
- The suitor will keep right on suiting. No matter what you do, this interloper will be able to take his shots from the gallery. In fact, your opponent may have read this book and had already explained to your employee all the reasons he should never accept a counteroffer. (See Chapter 4.)
- He resigned because you were unable to identify and meet several of his needs. If you couldn't identify them while he was your employee, you certainly won't be able to do so now. Even if you get lucky and do make him an offer that makes him reconsider, the chances are the real root of his dissatisfaction will remain and he'll leave (for good) within six months.
- Also, let's say you are successful in keeping him. What did you have to give him to make that happen? You may have made a long list of concessions and I'll bet one of those was a big chunk of cash. This whole event did not take place in a vacuum. The grapevine will assure all your employees knew he resigned and will soon know the details of how you saved him. What will be their response when learning how his compensation plan now compares to theirs? You may have (temporarily) saved one employee but you have permanently created a whole heap of problems with the rest of your team. ("The only way to get a raise around here is to quit!")

So, am I suggesting you just roll over and give up? Usually, yes. It is almost certainly too late and your efforts are rarely a good investment of your time (which is why I have placed so much emphasis on preventing the resignation rather than reacting to it). Even after all of my warnings, you still want to try? Good for you. I like your spirit. A bit naïve, perhaps, but you obviously have a wonderful attitude toward retention and I surely don't want to suppress that.

Consider these points before you attempt to save an employee who resigns:

1. If she just made her decision, then she may still be wavering. Make your attempt before her feet are set in concrete. Try to block those things that tend to lock in decisions, such as making an announcement. Ask her not to tell any fellow team members about her resignation until she has had a chance to think about it. This is important because an employee often wants to change her mind but doesn't want to lose face among her peers.
2. Understand that you must address *all* her concerns if you want to save her. It only takes one un-met need to generate a resignation, so don't try to keep her if you are unwilling to address every single issue.

Unfortunately, I must remind you that you will almost certainly lose this employee within the year. This is because no matter how sincere you have tried to address every need, some of the unspoken needs will remain. Since they were not uncovered, the frustrations will return.

Despite this sour prognosis, I do have some good news. I offer an effective strategy for dealing with employee resignations that may, in the long run, actually create a stronger and longer lasting relationship. So what do I suggest you do when an employee resigns? Let him. Then, follow my *Butterfly Strategy.*

THE BUTTERFLY STRATEGY FOR REVERSING RESIGNATIONS

Some of you may remember a poster from the mid-70s. Against a colorful background featuring a flittering butterfly it said, "If you love someone, set her free. If she comes back, she's yours, if she doesn't, she never was."

I have a better strategy for dealing with employee resignations; let me try to explain it as you wipe that tear from your eye. When an employee resigns, let her go. Wish her well, congratulate her on her good fortune, and even celebrate the achievement. Make it clear you appreciate all she has done and that the door will always be open; then, show her the door. Call her up about three months later. Ask how things are going and tell her she is missed. Let the conversation progress from there. If it was meant to be, it will be.

Why three months? As we learned in Chapter 5, this is a critical time for new employees. The luster has worn off both the job and the employee. The wonderful orientation and celebration are faded memories; she has settled into a routine, and may even be in a rut. She has probably entertained some second-thoughts about her decision to leave you. This is indeed the right time to counter-court her.

This is a much more effective way to retain a worker. While an employee who retracts a resignation will almost certainly leave you within a year, a rehired employee tends to stay with your company much longer than the average team members. Also, an important message is sent to the rest of your team: The grass is not greener over there, so don't even bother to look. Sarah did and chose to come back to her real home.

Rehiring a former employee has a much more positive impact on morale than negotiating with an employee to stay. Instead of workers being disheartened by all the concessions you gave up to keep her, they'll be motivated by the fact that she returned to her place on the team.

TURN FORMER EMPLOYEES INTO ALUMNI

"Can I take your order?" said a familiar voice from the drive-thru speaker. I had pulled in for a quick bag of cholesterol and recognized the voice as belonging to a former employee from many years before. In fact, that relationship had ended when I had to fire him for poor performance.

We both smiled when we met at the window and I greeted him with an enthusiastic "How are you doing!" He handed me my order and replied, "Well, I don't hate you anymore." I suddenly remembered why I had fired him. As I began to leave, I offered him some career advice: "Wow, Tim, you really ought to write greeting cards for Hallmark."

Most separations are unpleasant. Workers are often angry and contemptuous toward their former companies. Many employers look upon former employees as enemies, traitors, or, at the least, *persona non grata*. They are wiped from memory as quickly as they are dropped from the payroll. This is a terrible waste. Instead of severing contact, work to develop a solid business friendship. Instead of considering them ex-employees, learn to treat them as alumni.

While this positive relationship may be a challenge for some situations, for others this is a bit easier to do. Throughout the life of your business, you will have dynamic people who must leave in order to chase their own big dreams. A loyal worker will choose to be a full-time mom. Despite your best efforts, you will occasionally hire a talented professional who just wasn't a good match for the job. These wonderful people fall into that evil black hole we call turnover.

There are many advantages to shifting the perception of relationships. Most obvious is that by doing so you are leaving the door open for future employment. This may happen in the short-term, as described earlier, or it could happen later. Perhaps a clerk leaves you to take a bigger job elsewhere. They put him through school and, because you have maintained good relations, he eventually returns as your in-house attorney.

Alumni can help you even without ever being on your payroll again. They are a wonderful source of credible candidate referrals. They will often send new clients and customers to you (just as you did for them). I have seen some excellent employee development programs built using alumni as mentors.

Work hard to prevent turnover in your organization. When it does happen, separate on good terms. There was something that brought you and the employee together to start with; focus on that and work toward a mutually productive friendship as you both chase your dreams.

Much to my family's relief, I dealt with my midlife crisis in a positive manner. I dropped seventy pounds, converted the garage into a library, and ran for my first political office. (Stop whistling *Hail to the Chief*. Though I did win in a landslide, I now hold the lowest-ranking political office in the state of Georgia. Yes, the dogcatcher actually does outrank me.) However, I do still have my eye on that red sports car.

Many of your workers will not react so well to bumps in the road. They will have issues in their personal and professional lives and may choose to take all their problems out on you. Accept this as a part of doing business in the twenty-first century and learn how to manage these situations for the long haul.

Saving an employee in crisis is difficult, often impossible. That is why we have put so much emphasis on turnover prevention. Save all those you can, but never lose sight of the fact that the best way to stop turnover is to prevent it one at a time.

Coda: One at a Time

You didn't become a successful entrepreneur by following the crowd. You have avoided the well-trod paths and have learned to question much of the conventional wisdom that is tossed in your direction. So join me for a moment as we crumble the foundations of three pieces of conventional business wisdom.

BUT THERE IS IN *EQUIPO*

The instructor will pause for dramatic effect and then, with his face absolutely beaming, announce to those attending his teambuilding program: "Remember, there is no 'I' in team!"

Well, there should be. You are destined for frustration and failure if you attempt to build a team full of clones. A successful team can only exist if you celebrate the diversity of ideas, experiences, and perspectives. A team is a collection of I's who know how to work together and have been pointed in a worthwhile direction. The individual is the one absolute ingredient for a successful team.

But this really screws up a great cliché, doesn't it? Let me suggest a way to save it: Change it to Spanish. The Spanish word for team is *equipo*. What a great word for the concept. Not only does it include the word *I*, but it also contains the wonderfully apropos verb *equip*. My suggested replacement—my contribution to twenty-first century business clichés—"You can't spell *equipo* without an *I*."

OK, it'll never catch on and my future as a cliché writer appears dim indeed. However, I have succeeded on a more important level. You will never again listen to that old gem without remembering that you cannot have a true team unless you focus on the individual.

YOU ARE NOT MIKE

I tell the "Michael Jordan playing baseball" story (see Chapter 12) at most of my public appearances. This usually spawns a string of MJ stories from the audience. Eventually, one person will say, "Michael's secret of success is that he is not afraid to fail. He's willing to take risks most people wouldn't even consider." The audience will nod and accept this gem of wisdom.

I'm not impressed with this perspective, though. The fact is I would also be willing to try just about anything if I had half a billion dollars in my checking account.

Risk requires risk.

FORGET THE STUPID BOX

You know the activity. At the beginning of a "creative thinking" seminar, you are given a sheet of paper containing nine dots, arranged in three rows of threes. You are instructed to connect the dots by drawing no more than four straight lines without lifting the pencil from the paper. The solution, as you know by now, is to extend your lines past the square boundaries suggested by the dots, allowing you to approach from a different angle. The instructor will then announce that the exercise teaches us to "think outside the box."

I saw this exercise for the umpteenth time, so I decided to have a bit of fun and propose a few alternative solutions. One was to roll the paper into a cone and connect all the dots with just one spiraling line. Another involved folding the paper so all the dots lined up and then stab a pencil through the mass. Yet another option was to put the paper in a copy machine and reduce the picture to the point that the dots became one big blob that can be covered by a single stroke from a wide marker.

I pulled the instructor aside and smiled as I showed him my proposed solutions. "Oh no, Ken. That's not how it is done," he scolded. "You just listen up and I'll show you the proper way to solve the puzzle." I found irony in the fact that the most oft-used exercise for teaching people to think outside the box actually insists that participants adhere to a specific solution.

Here's the drill: Sometimes you should work outside the box. Sometimes you have to work inside the box. However, your best work comes when you realize there is no box. Reject any convention that goes against your guts. When developing your team, you are usually told to follow the exact recruiting template, mold everyone into clones, and treat everyone exactly the same. Your gut tells you this is wrong. Follow your gut.

A CLICHÉ I LIKE

A man walked onto a beach littered with hundreds—no, thousands—of starfish. They had been deposited by the tide hours before and were all facing certain death as they dried in the hot sun. As he looked up the beach, he saw a young girl picking up starfish and throwing them back in the ocean. "You're wasting your time," the man told the girl. There are just too many of them. What you are doing won't make any difference."

"It will to the ones I save," she responded.

The Entrepreneur's Guide to Eating Elephants explains that it is best done one bite at a time. It's the same with recruiting a team: *one person at a time.* It is how you build a team: *one individual at a time.* It is most certainly how you keep your team: *one at a time.*

Index

About the Author

KEN TANNER is a human resources consultant and expert in retention. An entrepreneur and former senior executive for both Taco Bell and Long John Silver's, he is the author of *Recruiting Excellence, Retaining Employees* and *Never Order Barbecue in Maine: Proven Career Strategies from People Who've Been There, Done That*.